THE PITTSBURGH THEOLOGICAL
MONOGRAPH SERIES

Dikran Y. Hadidian

General Editor

30

KARL BARTH IN RE-VIEW

Posthumous Works Reviewed and Assessed

KARL BARTH IN RE-VIEW
Posthumous Works Reviewed and Assessed

Edited by
H.-Martin Rumscheidt

With an Introduction by
Eberhard Busch
and
An Afterword by
Hans Frei

PICKWICK PUBLICATIONS
An imprint of *Wipf and Stock Publishers*
199 West 8th Avenue • Eugene OR 97401

Pickwick Publications
An imprint of Wipf and Stock Publishers
199 W 8th Ave, Suite 3
Eugene, OR 97401

Karl Barth In Re-View
Posthumous Works Reviewed and Assessed
Edited by Rumscheidt, H. Martin
Copyright©1981 Pickwick Publications
ISBN: 978-1-4982-2804-6
Publication date 1/1/1981

CONTENTS

PREFACE

On July 7, 1971 seven men founded the *Karl Barth Stiftung*:
Markus Barth, Alexander Bronkhorst, Georges Casalis, Max
Geiger, Walter Kreck, Frank Fischer, and Max Zellweger-Barth.
Their purpose was to give scope to the range and significance
of Barth's *entire* work, to collect and to preserve all the
literature by and about Barth, to prepare a complete edition
of Barth's writings and to support theological study and research which perceives itself in a biblical-evangelical and
ecumenical perspective. Clearly, a foundation with a momentous
aim.

Some months later, on October 28, 1972, the *Stiftung's*
sibling was born: the Karl Barth Society of North America.
Gathering for that society's first colloquium at Toronto,
well over 100 theologians, pastors, students and laypersons
approved the aims of the new organization. Through encouraging
a critical and constructive theology in continuity with the
work of Karl Barth, it desires to give assistance to the project of publishing a complete edition of Barth's writings and
establishing a collection or archive of "Barthiana", to organize various types of conferences to explore the resources of
Karl Barth's work for theology, and to create a centre in
North America for literature by and about Barth, a centre
available for students and researchers on this side of the
Atlantic.

The *Stiftung* in Europe has created a high visibility for
itself. In addition to annual colloquia at Leuenberg near
Basel, to which ever growing numbers of participants now go,
the publication of the complete edition has proceeded well.
Eberhard Busch relates the events of its birth in his remarkable introduction to this book. Thus far, eleven volumes of
the first series of books in the *Gesamtausgabe* have appeared.
None of the materials they contain, with the exception of some
of the Barth-Thurneysen letters, have been published before.
This book addresses itself to those eleven volumes. A second
series, containing newly edited works previously published but
now difficult to obtain, has been launched with the appearance
of a volume of sermons preached in the years from 1954 to 1967,

the last 32 sermons by Barth.

The Karl Barth Society of North America, meanwhile, has also been quite active. Two more colloquia at Toronto followed the one of 1972; regional groups have been or are being established and have had conferences, and admission as an affiliated society into the American Academy of Religion in 1975 has permitted each year since gatherings at the Academy's annual meeting. A small, albeit growing collection of literature by and about Barth is located in Toronto. And much of what was presented at the three Toronto colloquia has seen publication in the Canadian quarterly *Studies in Religion/Sciences Religieuses*. Indeed, the 1972 colloquium material is available in a monograph: *Footnotes to a Theology**.

Committed to promoting the complete edition of Barth's works, the Karl Barth Society of North America invited knowledgable persons to prepare shorter reviews of the *Gesamtausgabe* volumes for the above named quarterly *SR* as well as long reviews which, upon gathering, could serve as an introduction to some hitherto unknown aspects of Barth's work. It is with immense joy and gratitude that the KBSNA welcomes the inclusion of this review into the Pittsburgh Theological Monograph Series. The editor of The Pickwick Press reminded us constantly that personality-cults never served scholarship and theology well, but that critical engagement, be it interpretation of or dispute with Barth's thought, would serve the constructive task of theology. To that task this volume consciously wants to address itself and desires to participate in it, believing with Eberhard Jüngel that "Karl Barth gave much to his time. Thus far it has taken little from him. One suspects, therefore, that the future of his theology lies still quite far ahead of us."

From the days of his doctoral dissertation: *The Doctrine of Revelation in the Thought of Karl Barth 1909-1922*, onward Hans Frei has paid close attention to Barth's theology, that which Barth built on, rejected or influenced. The afterword to this volume, Frei's review of Eberhard Busch's biography of Barth, gives evidence to his long reflection on Barth and on what Barth has given to our time.

In a project like this one senses with special poignancy the reality and blessedness of interdependence. I have, as editor, the privileged obligation of expressing the gratitude

---

* Edited by H. Martin Rumscheidt; Wilfrid Laurier University Press; Waterloo, Ontario, 1974. ISBN 0-919812-02-3.

in which that blessedness is embedded. To my seven co-reviewers I say thank-you for their readiness to undertake the two-pronged task of assisting the editors of *SR* in their work of informing our 'guild' of the *Gesamtausgabe* and of preparing the reviews gathered here. To Eberhard Busch a thank-you and a bow for his thoughtful introduction. To Hans Frei go words of joy in welcoming him to this band of Barth 'amateurs'.

I am sure that all who read this volume will join in the gratitude given here to our copy-editor, Ms Liz McKee of Ottawa; she 'transfigured' much which, even though written in English, was still Teutonic. Lastly, thank-you, Dikran Hadidian, for the patience and encouagement with which you accompanied all this work. Let this book be dedicated to you with our appreciation.

Christmas 1980   H. Martin Rumscheidt
                                        Halifax, Nova Scotia

INTRODUCTION

"What I look for is understanding, not veneration."

Karl Barth

During a stroll from the Gianicolo to the Piazza Navona
in Rome, a Franciscan, particularly *au courant* about the literature of recent Protestant theology, told me: "I perceive
Karl Barth's works to be on a different plane than almost all
other Protestant literature of our century. For that reason,
I do not minimize in any way its significance, but Barth's
theology is distinguished from that literature, because it is,
simply, 'classic theology'--a theology of such weight and power,
of such consistency and consequence that to him, the Roman
Catholic, it is comparable only to the work of Thomas Aquinas".

I think I understand the comment that Barth's theology
is 'classic theology;' it is an impression and a judgment I
share. Barth occasionally remarked of Calvin's theology that,
even with its clearly problematic aspects, it has 'metallic
substance' (a theology, let it be noted, Barth did not face
uncritically). And the same can be said of his theology. It is
not made of sugar. It is neither cheap throw-away-plastic, nor
imitation, but has 'metallic substance.' It is 'real stuff,'
simply, 'classic theology.' Occupying oneself with it is like
entering a beautiful, solemn, spacious church where although
attention is paid to the issues of the day, the day's prattle
may be left behind. Singleminded devotion to the worship alone
of God is found there, irrespective of one's desire to enter
into or remain aloof from it.

It is a church in which things proceed very much as they
did in the Roman Catholic house of God during World War I of
which Barth later wrote with so much respect. "The chanting
of the *Magnificat* continued without distraction and interrup-
tion, even though a shell had crashed through the roof."[1] What
characterizes this theology is that, while modern, it looks
with disdain at theological vagaries of fashion, currently ram-
pant. It abstains from subjective arbitrariness and outpour-
ings, even where it speaks in language personally engaged and
grasped; it resists handy buzzwords and phrases even in its
basic discussion. It is a theology which, even when pursuing
most intricate, specific points to their smallest detail, does
not lose itself in side-issues or peculiarities. It never remains at the surface, but always goes to the root of things and
by seeking what is basic still weighs possible and necessary
consequences. It has before it the one and the whole of faith
in that it focuses in every instance on it through one, particular, concrete aspect. It touches no detail, however minute,
without ever losing sight of the whole of faith. It says always the same by ever again saying it differently in rich diversity and it always says it differently by really saying the
same every time in great simplicity. In each specific instance
it espouses a particular insight without, at the same time,
giving up its own position. Continuously *en route*, it steadily
proceeds forward in a long march, never darting about without
aim or out of breath. It is of one cast, even where its
cracks show and where it corrects itself; it is, again, of one
cast precisely by not becoming a 'system' or, what is worse, a
game with principles. Even when it is occupied with complicated
movements of thought, this theology does not lack the child-
likeness of faith; setting out consciously from faith, it does
not despise thinking, does not shun comprehension but, instead,
presses persistently, yes, impetuously for understanding, for

intelligibility, for 'enlightenment'. It does not try to avoid problems but has, at the same time, the courage to leave otherwise much discussed 'issues' aside because it believes that it has to deal with more urgent and important things. When addressing itself directly to contemporary society it does not seek to create an effect nor does it play with words when reflecting on the mysteries of the divine being. It takes its own era seriously, yes, but it acts far more like the needle of a compass than a weather-vane. When speaking of 'the eternal truths' it does not leave the impression that its words are uttered from the relaxed musings in an arm-chair but that they come from the trenches of the *ecclesia militans*. It perceives itself as a 'free science' by wanting to be bound completely and fundamentally to its object of cognition. By being bound to its object, this theology is made free to incorporate in an eclectic manner the thinking of the most diverse theological as well as non-theological minds. This theology is entirely devoted to its subject-matter although it seriously asks itself whether its efforts in thinking might not be flight from the living God. By being self-critical and suspicious toward its own logic, its own 'point of departure', it is at the very same time quite sure of its subject, raising serious questions but not doubting, speaking with differentiation but not with reservation. In short: while it can be calmly admitted with him who fashioned it, that this theology has problematic aspects, it does have 'metallic substance', is of 'real stuff', is 'classic theology', a claim one cannot make for much of the theology before, next to, and after Karl Barth.

When I call it classic theology, I do not mean that it is 'conservative', 'restoration', 'scholastic', or 'neo-orthodox' theology, or whatever else it has been called along this line. In the second and third generations after Barth there is some bewilderment that so many of the generation immediately after him, regardless of whether they agreed with him or not, often read and understood him in such a way. However divided the prominent representatives of more recent Barth-interpretation may be as to *what* was the truly novel element in his thought, they are at one *that* something new did enter the theological plane with it. This they now assert with the almost impetuous joy of discovery in the face of much of what had hitherto been said about the work of Barth. Almost too strongly, they emphasize what is 'modern' in it (let us call it that for now) and his iconoclastic relation to the whole of tradition of church and theology, a relation where not one stone is left standing on another. There is Eberhard Jüngel, citing the radical break with metaphysics by that equally radical relational understanding of how the free God and the free human being encounter each other. Friedrich Wilhelm Marquardt calls attention to the fundamentally new orientation of the whole of theological reflection resulting from a social-materialistic view of reality. Trutz Rendtorff points to the radicalization of the idea of autonomy in Barth's thought in the sense of a fulfillment of the Enlightenment.

Whatever one might think of each of these daring theses individually, they do elicit the suprising hunch that the bases are meagre indeed for relegating this theologian to the ranks of the behind-the-times descendants of medieval architects of thought-edifices or that his theology is repristination of a '*theologia perennis*'. Barth's theology has plowed new furrows in its field indeed. Something, however, which belongs to the "classical" of his theology is that it understands itself essentially as 'church' theology. Nothing could be more odd than to qualify that as 'restorative'. In this sense of *church* theology, it is indeed not a 'conservative' theology nor, for that matter, a 'revolutionary' theology. And if it does plough new furrows it does so not in the proud-despairing self-consciousness of the isolated individual thinking for her/ himself, but in the far-reaching, decisive self-understanding of being one among other members of the church of Jesus Christ. Here Barth's thought breaks with Neo-Protestant theologizing. His relation to the tradition of church and theology was both positively and critically influenced by this self-understanding as was, of course, his perception of the nature of the scientific task and responsibility of theology. Not unaware of the problematic of their particular historical development, Barth regarded the documents of that tradition as more than mere testimonies of 'the past' but, since faith in the resurrection had to prove itself here too, as present and living witnesses of the church of Jesus Christ. This signified a break with one of the typical 'doctrines' of Neo-Protestantism, according to which the onset of the modern world brought in its train a most fateful determination of Christian faith which has now made the church's witness of 'pre-modern times' simply obsolete. It meant, at the same time, a remarkably wide openness on Barth's part to a plenitude of older and ancient traditions of church and theology. Insights almost forgotten or relegated into dusty attics were brought forward again and taken seriously. What other theology embodies such a multiplicity of traditional statements, traditional in the truest sense of 'handed on', as does this one? True, Barth dealt freely with all traditions. If he preferred that of the Reformers, it was not without an increasingly sharp critical view of their limitations. If he repudiated that view of Neo-Protestantism, it was not without enquiring to the very end, and with a sense of disquiet, after its nevertheless legitimate concern. None of these traditions he treated uncritically but applied the advice that everything should be tested and the best kept. His criterion of testing was not how 'relevant' to our time a tra-

ditional assertion was but how 'appropriate' to its object. I
would like to think of this unique combination of taking traditions seriously while remaining free before them, as a sign of
the "classical" of Barth's theology.

I see the truly classic aspect of that theology in its
powerful and insistent calling of church and theology to 'the
heart of the matter'. It was a most characteristic call, made
ever more sharply, so that it would indeed call Barth's own
theology, too, to that 'heart'.

I could put it this way: the specific way of its theologizing is what is truly classic in Barth's theology. The sentence *"Human beings know God in that they stand before God"*[2]
indicates with brevity that specific way. If read carefully
and interpreted correctly, it sounds a whole range of positive
theses and negative antitheses characteristic of Barth--the repudiation of Neo-Protestant subjectivism. According to it,
God is 'something' of the human, so that to speak of God means
really that we humans once again speak of ourselves in elevated
tones. Instead, argues Barth, God is different from us. He
remains the one who is over-against us (*unser Gegenüber*), beyond our disposition precisely by being turned toward and known
by us. Rejection of a metaphysics which seems to know of an
abstract, object-like being of God! Instead, argues Barth,
and everything depends on this, God is by nature the one who
turns toward human beings and meets them and that concretely,
factually. Delimitation against every form of apologetics!
One cannot prove that God is and that there is knowledge of
God; one can only come again and again to God's reality and
give one's testimony to it. One can see from that sentence the
rejection of natural theology so important for Barth. A natural theology that somehow speculates on an abstract 'precondition' to the situation described in that sentence, in which
God encounters human beings who, standing before God, know God.

The rejection, in other words, of a theology which either
alleges a knowledge of God independent of the concrete situation or posits a capacity in human being for entering into it,
a capacity 'distilled' from human nature *per se*. Both are repudiated by that sentence: only he is God who gives himself
to be known by encountering human beings and who thereby becomes encountered by them.

There is, correspondingly, no other capacity to know God
than that which they, without having it beforehand, are in
fact given in the occurrence of God's self-giving for their
knowledge.

Something else one can hear from that sentence, something
which from his middle period onward Barth impressed upon himself more and more rigorously: the critique of the conception
of preaching which saw preaching as having a mediating-
instrumental function. He extended that critique to similar
conceptions of the sacraments, of any activity of the church,
of Christianity and theology, yes, to any such conceptions of
the church itself. This critique seeks decisively to prevent
people from departing from that situation of being before God
in their activities and existence which such a conception
would cause. They depart from it and cast it behind their
backs in the belief of standing on God's side, of having the
divine at their disposition and being able to mediate, apply
or transform it. For Barth, on the other hand, the Holy
Spirit alone is *mediator* of salvation in the actual sense of
that term. Human beings, meanwhile, in all their ecclesial,
Christian and theological activities can always only *remain*
standing in that situation of being before God. Therefore, in
all those activities and, hence, in continuous solidarity with
other human beings, that is, without ever being able to leave
it behind, they can be only witnesses, in the strictest sense
of the word. The sentence, that human beings know God in that
they stand before God, contains *in nuce* an entire theology.

What is equally important to me is that it also depicts the
specific *position* in which Barth sought to develop and present
his theology. He once depicted it as the first, concrete formal principle of theology which must be considered and respected throughout: the "biblical character" in theology. This
does not refer to simple biblicism, but to a structure of
thought which joins itself to the manner of speaking seen in
the biblical authors. "They are witnesses. But that means
that they are not observers, reporters, dialecticians, parti-
sans". It is a manner in which one fundamentally does not
speak 'about' God; what is said about God is not done with constant side-glances elsewhere but *face to face* with God.[3] Something else is at issue here, namely what Barth called the
"ecclesial character" of theology. No ecclesiasticism is implied here, nor a sanctioning of the church's empirical existence (especially not that!) nor a thinking which sees its task
in justifying itself before the forum of a general, even academic, consciousness of culture. He means a thinking which
understands itself as service in and for the church of Jesus
Christ, and which focusses centrally on its worship of God
and, in that way, is itself a part of that worship on the
plane of thinking. In other words, Barth is deeply concerned
to 'do' a kind of theology which does its work "in the act of
prayer", work whose "*laborare* itself, and as such, is essentially an *orare*".[4] By tackling its work in this sense, by thinking
through Christian theology in a new way from root to highest
twig in this spirit Barth's theology became and was *classic*
theology.

———————

Precisely this expression "classic theology" was used in
a significant moment a year and a half after Barth's death. In
July 1970, some of his friends from Germany, France and Switzer-

land had come together near Basel to discuss what and how much of his unpublished literary legacy to publish, no matter what the obstacles might be. The wise *Dogmatiker* and historian of doctrine, Ernst Wolf of Göttingen, who also is dead now, made the following suggestion in a daring proposal: regarding a posthumous publication of Barth's writings, there can really be no question of a selection from them, nor a mere edition of the unpublished works left behind. There has to be nothing less than a complete edition of all of Barth's published and unpublished works, a *Gesamtausgabe* analagous to the *Weimar Edition* of Luther's works. For, his theology is classic theology, Wolf said, comparable in its rank to Luther's, and its equal. Wolf's proposal eventually turned the scale and gave the impetus to plan for the proposed idea and to seek at least an approximate realization. It was surmised that some 60 to 70 volumes would be involved, perhaps even more. There was reasonable certainty that a task was envisaged which would take more than a hundred years to be completed. The next year, the *Karl Barth Stiftung* was founded. Its chief aim to raise the necessary capital for the preservation and publication of the literary legacy, especially of the unpublished material. Barth's last home in Basel, Bruderholzallee 26, was made available by his children for the establishment of the Karl Barth Archive in which all that material is housed. The house also serves as residence for an archivist, a position filled since its inception with great care by Dr. Hinrich Stoevesandt. Since them, several experts, using the standards of scientific editing, have begun to prepare texts from several stages of Barth's life for publication. The task of deciphering the manuscripts is arduous at times. Their work has taken longer than expected but in the decade since Barth's death, 12 volumes, comprising some 6400 pages, have already appeared. Such an enlargement of the already available corpus of Barth's makes great demands on the reader, not to say that it is an imposition. After all, there are the nearly 10,000 pages of the *Church Dogmatics* and the bibliography of his works published during his lifetime runs to nearly 600 titles. The justification, then, for such a truly demanding undertaking, one taxing especially the readers' world, can only be in something the above discussion tried to make reasonably clear: this theology deserves to become known and more of it than is presently the case. The point of this assertion is also that more attention might be paid to those works by Barth which appeared during his lifetime than is the case at present. He once made the somewhat mocking remark that "not everyone who thinks he is able to know and say all sorts of things about me has fulfilled even this condition"[5]--namely, to have read his work. How salutory it would be were this rule to govern the study of Barth's works: the principal and decisive texts according to which he wanted and, in all fairness, ought to be understood, are those writings he authorized for publication. What has to be kept in mind about the material not published when he died is that for various reasons and for a good part he consciously chose *not* to publish them. The decision he poured over the unpublished products of the previous ten years of his life was clearly more than a passing mood. He wrote to Eduard Thurneysen in 1928 that they were "overaged cheese" which made him "sick and shudder"; "you could light a huge bonfire with them. . ., your son Mathias ought to make paperplanes from the paper and the. . .sheets would serve toilet purposes well."[6] And yet these words serve as a reminder that the works Barth himself published should be read as primary texts which realistically deserve to be studied first and to be understood first. Still, Barth did not consign that unpublished material to that "bonfire" nor the material he was to add in subsequent years. He carefully preserved it instead.

xix

He did not rule out posthumous publication. What is more, the primary text has such a format that it deserves not only to be studied as such but, for the sake of a closer, better, more deeply penetrating, positive or critical understanding, also to be illumined and commented upon through knowledge of the material he did not publish.

I suspect or certainly hope that, in attempting to understand Barth, the use of the hitherto unpublished material will on the whole lead to questions which go in these two directions. The one aim, of course, for a better understanding of Karl Barth and his work which, no matter how one twists and turns it, is to be found chiefly in the *Church Dogmatics*. A series of specific questions becomes acute on account of the availability of the unpublished literary legacy. *For one*: what led him to write this *magnum opus*? Here the voluminous material from his early days becomes interesting: more than 500 sermons, his scientific addresses, his socialist speeches of his days as minister in Geneva and Safenwil (1909-1921), those youthful dramas of still earlier days composed in the spirit of Schiller, and his student essays written under Harnack and Herrmann. There are the many lectures in Exegesis, History of Theology, and Ethics given when he was a young professor at Göttingen and Münster (1921-1930). What caused the dedicated supporter of modern liberal theology to become an equally dedicated supporter of socialism? And then, after that 'prehistory', what made him write the first edition of his *Römerbrief* (1919) which represents such a sharp break with so much ecclesial-theological tradition and his own background, to be followed only by that completely recast second edition of 1922? Or what made him declare in the later twenties that he would stop "remaining in the posture of a prophet in which, so it seems, some people have seen me for a moment or two" and be, instead, "an ordinary theologian who does not have the word of

God at his disposition but, at best, a 'Doctrine of the Word of God'." What was the reason that he broke off his endeavour to write a 'Christian Dogmatics' only to begin anew in 1932, during his time at Bonn (1930-1935), with the 'Church Dogmatics'? The complete edition, now in process of publication, promises significant help precisely for such questions. But the most exciting of them will be this: are the documents from the early period evidence of different possibilities, closed to him later, of going about the task of theology other than the one he felt he had to pursue in the *CD*? Or, are there stages on a way on which, given all the changes, the earlier is somehow preserved in the later, as Rendtorff maintains regarding liberalism and Marquardt regarding socialism? Sharper still and in more rudimentary fashion: are the earlier texts 'preliminary material' to the *CD* which Barth rejected with justification? Or even: are they, apart from that later work, to be seen as theological experiments and beginnings which have their own intrinsic merit and which could be held up critically against his later work?

Another series of questions is this: how did Barth attend to his great, chief work, first at Bonn and then at Basel (from 1935 onward)? And how did he look back on what he wrote there and from there later? A whole range of fragments are important here: shorter and longer texts composed for the *CD* but removed from the manuscripts before publication, texts which as such bring the reader much closer to the work-bench on which this dogmatics was fashioned. Part of them are the fragments for what would have been his final volume, IV/4, the ethics of reconciliation, a section of which Barth deliberately published, namely the doctrine of baptism, while equally as deliberately not publishing the rest.[3] Barth's 'conversations' from his last years after retirement from his academic position, the public discussions he had with several groups in which, re-

sponding directly to questions and critiques, he looks both
back and ahead in time, they, too, will be of interest here.[9]
So will be the documents from his seminar-sessions, in which,
in addition to lecturing, Barth often engaged in 'theology in
dialogue' with his students, having lively debates based on
old as well as more recent texts. One wonders whether Bonhoeffer's statement about Barth's seminars will prove true in
relation to these documents.

> "Barth is even better than his books.
> There is an openness, a willingness to
> listen to relevant criticism, and at the
> same time such an intensity of concentra-
> tion on and impetus pressing for the subject
> which can be discussed proudly or with modes-
> ty, dogmatically or with tentativeness, and
> it is certainly not meant primarily to serve
> his own theology."[10]

Then, there are the collections of observations, dating from
the days of Hitler and afterwards, which Barth made about current affairs and especially political matters, many of which
observations are still unknown. They will most likely intensi-
fy, and one hopes help answer more clearly, the question as to
what place and impact the political dimension had in his theology and what internal reference politics had to it.

And one *further* question: who was this man who gave us
this theology? More can be said about this when the voluminous body of Barth's letters will be fully available; four
volumes have already appeared. But, clearly there are other
perspectives from which to read these letters. There are letters devoted entirely or almost entirely to theological discussion; others are full of pastoral admonition and counsel;
others are comments on specific issues in church and politics
while still others are a kind of 'diary', like those to his
friend Thurneysen and, later, to his sons. But precisely in

these letters the person who wrote that theology emerges more
openly. And one can say even now that a rather unique figure
will become visible there, someone in whom tenderness and
harshness, merriment and a readiness to do battle, openness
and reserve, attentiveness and withdrawal, boyish flippancy
and adult charm, painful questioning and unbended confidence,
modesty and a full-blown self-consciousness were closely side
by side, rubbing one against the other. Here, too, all sorts
of questions will arise, especially about the relation of
biography and theology. In short, the appearance of the
Gesamtausgabe and, especially, of the hitherto unknown material could and should lead to a more vigorous, more differen-
tiated and also more insightful enquiry about the real meaning
of Barth's theology. One wonders with a good deal of antici-
pation whether, to be precise: how the understanding of his
theology will become clearer, deeper or be made more complicated given these kinds of questions, whether, to be precise:
how that understanding will change.

But I really would like now to assume and to suppose--I
certainly hope and wish earnestly--that the appearance of the
complete edition, including the unpublished literary legacy,
will lead to a study that will not exhaust itself in the pur-
suit of Karl Barth and his work, a direction in which the
questions above indeed tended to point. I hope and wish that
the already available and the planned volumes will lead to
questions going also in the opposite direction, the one,
namely, in which we are not the ones who do the asking but are
the ones being put to the question. I am convinced that
Barth's theology has both the format and the authority to
cause such reverse-questioning. I think that particularly
Barth's work cannot be read and understood sensibly and adequately if all our questions to him and his work fail to be
joined by that question of today's and tomorrow's theologians

which asks simply, straightforwardly and radically: are you
about the real issue or are you skylarking, no matter whether
you do it with or without depth, in conservative or modern
style? It is in this sense that I understand the remark Barth
made late in his life: "What I look for is understanding, not
veneration". Clearly, Barth wanted theologians after him to
reflect not with a view to him and his work, but with a living
relation to *that subject,* that issue in relation to which he
himself tried to do theology. Doing theology in relation to
Barth could mean doing it in an unfree subservience, causing
what one says to become a recital of what he said. He once
made the biting comment about so-called 'Barthians' who do
theology in that fashion. "If you meet any of them, give them
my regards and tell them that I am not a 'Barthian.'" Doing
theology in relation to *him* could, however, also mean that,
perhaps with polite bows to him and his work, one must absolutely say things differently from him. Those to whom this
may concern should consider his psychologically astute remark
about the younger Blumhardt, made while he himself was still a
young man: "what is so unique about the younger Blumhardt is
that [sc. in relation to his father] he precisely did *not* desire or have to be unique as is the wont of sons in relation
to their fathers."[11] Karl Barth did not wish to be 'venerated',
in the sense that he and his theology became the subject matter
of any theology, neither in an uncritical nor in a critical
form. But he wanted to be 'understood' which meant for him
that one became someone (and in this sense only followed Barth)
who was at work in confrontation with the 'issue', the 'subject
matter' with which he, Barth, found himself confronted in his
thinking. Or, to put it in form of a picture: the decisive
realization which dawned on him while he was yet a young minister at Safenwil, one which never let go of him but moved him
again and again, was that the figure of John the Baptist, as
depicted so impressively on the painting of the Isenheim Altar,

was really exemplary. This realization allowed his thought to become 'classic theology', that man who "with his hand points in an almost impossible way", or still more accurately, that "hand which is in evidence in the Bible".[12]

In all its different phases Barth's theology really wanted to be an endeavour to make way and to create space for a thinking in both theology and church which tries ever anew to be like that pointing hand, that movement which directs attention away from itself to the revealed God. His theology can rightly claim that about itself. To understand it, then, would mean accordingly that one would not come to a halt and contemplate *Barth's* 'pointing hand' by itself and as such, whether in an accepting or critical manner is beside the point. For that would be tantamount to 'venerating' his person or his teaching. To understand his theology would be to follow in the *direction* the Baptist's hand indicates, to turn toward the subject-matter it was concerned with. Appropriate critique of his theology would mean, accordingly, to concentrate on the question whether or where Barth's hand did not adequately point away from itself and in that direction. It would equally be a critical probing of one's own pointing and the subsequent endeavour to point away from oneself better and to become more like the hand of the biblical witness. What must be noted about this theology and its self-understanding as such a 'pointing' theology is that one really does not understand nor critique it appropriately if one fails to open oneself to critical enquiry, to the question: are you keeping to the point? Does your hand resemble that of the Baptist?--This, in essence, was his critique of Neo-Protestantism: according to all appearances, that finger was to all intents and purposes turned around by 180° and now pointed very much to the human instead of away from it or that it was made to point in any desired--and possibly quite undetermined direction other than that of the Baptist which pointed to the 'Word made flesh'.

With this in mind I ask whether it is a mistaken impression that, on the whole, theology has moved by Karl Barth relatively unscathed in this so important and critical matter. Has theology, in relation to his theology, not satisfied itself in finding, or missing, this or that 'tidbit', in seeking out Barth's rootage in Kant, or in Hegel, etc., something no one with a good mind would ever dispute?

Is it a mistaken impression that theology, to some extent already during Barth's life but more so since his death, has allied itself again to that tradition of Neo-Protestantism and sailed right on it, undisturbed by Barth's critical appeals?

Is it a mistaken impression that theology now takes it almost for granted again that the human: human characteristics and capacities, human needs and utopias, is the subject-matter of theology?

Is it a mistaken impression that another attempt is being made to reduce revelation to a manageable formula (all the while mistaking or even ignoring its mysterious nature), a formula which actually serves to legitimize a previously established anthropological interest?

Is it a mistaken impression that, for that reason, salvation is said to be found in historicism, or in religionism, or in ethicism (all the way down to crude works-righteousness), that it is to be found in sticking with concerns of methodology or in the drive toward the legitimization of theological science by approximating theology to all sorts of other sciences?

Is it or is it not so? If it is so, should it be so or not? A study of Barth's theology cannot be initiated while one is confronted by the fundamental and unambiguous critique raised by his understanding of theology and the disquieting, probing question: are you about the real thing?

Now that the complete edition is being published I do hope this question will be plainly put to both the current and next generation of theologians. Yes, I hope that 'we' find ourselves invited by it to pay heed to the invitation and admonition which Karl Barth addressed to 'us' after his retirement: "Let everyone do what I have tried to do, even much better than I, to the glory of God and of the neighbor."[13]

Eberhard Busch

NOTES

1. *The Word of God and the Word of Man,* (Boston, The Pilgrim Press, 1928), p. 112f.

2. *Church Dogmatics* II/1, (Edinburgh, T. and T. Clark, 1957), p. 9. This work will be cited as *CD* from now on. – Note: The editor has attempted to remove what a growing number of theologians perceive as non-inclusive language. This has caused slight discrepancies from the printed text.

3. *CD* I/2, pp. 816f.

4. *Evangelical Theology--An Introduction,* (Grand Rapids, Wm. B. Eerdmans Publishing Co., 1979), p. 160.

5. Weber, Otto, *Karl Barth's Church Dogmatics--An Introductory Report on Volumes* I/1 to III/4, (Philadelphia, The Westminster Press, 1953), p. 9.

6. *Karl Barth-Eduard Thurneysen Briefwechsel,* ed. by Eduard Thurneysen, vol. 2, (Zurich, TVZ, 1974), p. 606. (From the volumes reviewed by James Smart, *infra* pp. 55-64.

7. The allusion is to the title of the 'early' dogmatics Barth published, of which he never allowed a second edition. *Christliche Dogmatik im Entwurf, Die Lehre vom Worte Gottes.* (Munich, Chr. Kaiser Verlag, 1927). The cited material is from the Foreword, p. ix.

8. Much of the rest was published in vol. 7 of the *Gesamtausgabe*, which Charles Dickinson reviews, *infra*. pp. 43-54.

9. This volume is still in preparation. A sample may be found in Barth's *Fragments Grave and Gay*, ed. by H. M. Rumscheidt, (London, Collins, 1971), pp. 71ff.

10. In Bethge, Eberhard, *Dietrich Bonhoeffer*, (New York, Harper and Row, 1977), p. 132. The translation was amended to match more accurately the German original. (Ed. note.)

11. In *Vergangenheit und Zukunft*, (1919) cited in Moltmann, Jürgen (ed.) *Anfänge der dialektischen Theologie*, Vol. 1, (Munich, Chr. Kaiser Verlag, 1962), p. 45.

12. *The Word of God and the Word of Man*, p. 65.

13. From Barth's circular letter of 1961, in Karl Barth, *Briefe 1961-1968*, Jürgen Fangmeier and Hinrich Stoevesandt, eds., (Zürich, TVZ, 1975), p. 2. This is the volume reviewed by James Buckley, *infra*. pp. 83-93.

I: SERMONS

The Sermons of 1913 and 1914*

Arthur C. Cochrane

Series One of the Complete Edition, to include
only previously unpublished materials, is divided into six categories: sermons, academic
lectures, addresses and smaller studies, conversations, letters and biographica. Since
preaching was for Barth that which theology,
as a discipline, was to serve chiefly, the
planners of the Edition decided to devote the
first category to this, but also of subsequent,
series to Barth's sermons. It is appropriate,
therefore to place this review at the beginning.

Following a year as assistant minister under Adolf Keller
in Geneva, Barth served as pastor of an agricultural and indus-
trial community in Safenwil, Canton of Aargau, from 1911 to
1921. During this period he delivered close to 500 sermons.
After extensive preparation they were carefully written down
word for word. Once on paper, Barth believed that he could defend them theologically but he often felt that homiletically

---

*Karl Barth, *Predigten 1913*, Nelly Barth and Gerhard Sau-
ter, eds., (Zürich, TVZ, 1976). p. 719; *Predigten 1914*. Ursala
and Jochen Fähler, eds., (Zürich, TVZ, 1974), p. 666. These
two volumes 8 and 5 in the *Gesamtausgabe*.

they were not satisfactory and wished that he could have re-
written them, even after several rejected attempts. Barth
seldom corrected his final manuscripts and, therefore, a reading of his sermons gives no idea of the toil that led up to
their final form. At first he closely followed his manuscripts.
Later, he was able to deliver his sermons more freely.

Barth did not follow a lectionary nor did he preach from
a particular book of the Bible. Contrary to the advice he
once gave in lectures on preaching, he usually selected brief
texts. Occasionally he would preach a series of sermons on a
certain passage, as for example, Amos 3:1-8; 5:4; 18-20;
Matthew 4:18-20 in 1913, and six sermons on Romans 1:16, another six on Matthew 26:17 to 27:50, and four on Matthew 6:33
in 1914. Of the 50 sermons delivered in 1913, 33 of the texts
were chosen from the New Testament, the remainder from the Old.
In 1914 the ratio was 35 to 18 in favour of the New.

Eberhard Busch informs us that when Barth began preaching,
he frequently delivered topical sermons on such subjects as
'Prayer', 'Reformation', 'Pride', 'Mission' and 'The Life of
William Booth'.[1] By 1913 this type of preaching had been
abandoned and the preacher is conscious that the sermon must
be bound by the text.

On the other hand, Barth's sermons were by no means
purely expository. He strove to develop central themes or
concepts in a text in order to address the concrete situations
in the life of his parishioners, the church, society and the
world. His purpose was to enlarge the horizon of the congregation and to increase its awareness in terms of the reality
of the living God which included world-events as signs and
admonitions. Those who heard him were to learn to look beyond
their immediate experiences and to see them in the light of
their deepest dimensions and implications. In this way Barth
uttered a prophetic message against dependence on material

things, Mammonism, the cruelty of child labour, neglect of
education in the schools, alcoholism, and the inhumanity of
prevailing economic and social conditions.

At that time, Barth was involved in socialism and especially the trade union movement. This is evident from his
sermons, especially those on the Book of Amos. Yet it is
doubtful whether he was ever an ideological socialist. He
took stands on social and economic issues as the need arose.
Characteristically, he joined the Socialist Party in Switzerland after he had soundly criticized it. In a lecture on
"Gospel and Socialism", delivered February 1, 1914, he stated:
"I regard socialist demands as an important part of the ap-
plication of the gospel, though I also believe that they cannot be realized without the gospel."

What, then, is the theology that forms the basis of these
sermons? They belong to the period of Barth's liberalism when
he was still very much under the influence of Schleiermacher
and Kant. In 1912 he had lauded the former as "the brilliant
leader of a new reformation". Consequently terms such as
'life', 'experience', 'the inner man', and 'conscience' (which
was virtually synonymous for 'revelation' as the voice of God
in us) occur frequently. A sermon on Acts 17:26-28 defines
God as the one upon whom we are absolutely dependent, who is
immanent in us and is known in our conscience and experience.
God is equated with the highest and best in our souls. It is
clear in these sermons that Barth had not yet discarded his
theological beginnings and had not arrived at a sense of the
discontinuity of a way from the human to God. The person of
Jesus is central. Indeed, Barth appears to have been fasci-
nated by this strange man. Yet obviously, we do not have the
christological precision concerning what God has said and done
in Jesus Christ which we encounter in the *Church Dogmatics* and
his later sermons. On the contrary, we find a moral influence

theory of Jesus' deeds and words which serves to increase our faith and to inspire our consciences and wills.

Does this mean that these sermons can have only an anti-quarian or historical interest for us? Do they simply present positions which Barth later repudiated and abandoned? Or is the case such that in spite of their liberal trappings we may find in these sermons a witness to the truth attested to in Scripture which is relevant to our situation today? Is there a message both comforting and edifying? Whatever fears one may have had were dispelled. First of all, one sees in these sermons a man strenuously wrestling with Scripture, even with passages that appear to contradict common sense and experience, and struggling to hear what is being said. As a result, the gospel repeatedly comes through loud and clear. The unity of God's grace and holiness, of his mercy and righteousness, which years later Barth was to work out in his doctrine of God, is reaffirmed and illustrated. It is this feature which dis-tinguishes Barth's 1913-1914 sermons from the moralism and religiosity that have characterized both liberal and conserva-tive sermons in America.

These bulky volumes will probably never be translated and it is unrealistic to hope than an English edition of the ser-mons Barth delivered from August 2 through December 27, 1914 will be published. They represent a massive theological cri-tique of World War I and of the racism, nationalism, and struggle for economic and political power that gave rise to it. Yet, in spite of their stern note of judgment, these sermons offered tremendous comfort for a bewildered and fearful people. What a pity they were not widely read during and after that War and were, instead, virtually buried in a village in Swit-zerland! What a pity they are not available in English to those of us who live under the threat of a nuclear holocaust.

It has often been said that the outbreak of World War I

was the occasion, if not the cause, of Barth's break with liberal, cultural Protestantism. He himself has admitted that
the War was a shattering experience. He was shocked by Germany's violation of Belgium's neutrality, but even more by the
fact that all of his theological professors in Germany, had
subscribed to a manifesto endorsing the Kaiser's war policy.[2]

What gave rise to Barth's disillusionment with the theological, ecclesiastical, cultural, and humanist spirit of the
times? From the 1913-1914 sermons I am persuaded his disen-
chantment arose from the fact that the God whose voice he was
hearing in Scripture was not the God to whom all the warring
nations, including their churches, were praying for victories
over their enemies. He was not the God of the so-called
Christian West. The War prompted Barth to probe more deeply
and to call into question the exegetical, dogmatic, and ethical presuppositions that prevailed in Protestantism and Roman
Catholicism, but as a preacher, who was called upon to expound
Scripture for his congregation from Sunday to Sunday, he had
already embarked upon such a probing. God's Word was raising
questions concerning a world at war. Barth's later theology
represents answers wrung from the same Word which had posed
the questions. Herein lies the evangelical character of these
volumes of sermons and, therefore, their enduring importance.

NOTES

1. Busch, Eberhard, *Karl Barth--His life from letters and autobiographical texts,* (Philadelphia, Fortress Press, 1976), p. 62.

2. For the text of the manifesto see Rumscheidt, Martin, *Revelation and Theology--An Analysis of the Barth-Harnack Correspondence of 1923,* (London, Cambridge University Press, 1972), p. 202-203.

II: ACADEMIC LECTURES

1. Ethics *

Paul L. Lehmann

Barth's academic lectures will have their place in the second category of all series of the Complete Edition. Four of his 'courses' will occupy us in this section.--
The lectures on Ethics are the first to be addressed, even though they were given later than those on Schleiermacher and John's Gospel. Presented during the summer and winter semesters of 1928-1929 at Münster and repeated two years later at Bonn, these lectures took shape in the Germany shaped by that war the outbreak of which so drastically shaped Barth's sermons of late 1914. In addition, there are now clear signs of the emergence of a theology and ethics which are not rooted in the traditions Barth felt compelled to break away from in 1914 but which were still strongly present in prevalent German Protestant theology in the late twenties.
Lehmann gave this subtitle to his review: The conceptuality, content, and concreteness of Christian ethics theologically considered.

Karl Barth came to Münster on October 25, 1925, after

four years in Göttingen. On October 13, 1921 he had "left the

---

*Karl Barth, *Ethik* I, Dietrich Braun, ed. (Zürich, TVZ, 1973, pp. 435; *Ethik* II, Dietrich Braun, ed. (Zürich, TVZ, 19 1978, pp. 504. These two volumes are numbers 2 and 10 in the *Gesamtausgabe*.

7

beautiful Aargau and joined 'the Swiss on foreign service'."[1]
In Göttingen he had begun his systematic attention to dogmatics
which he continued at Münster and which was published as *Die
Christliche Dogmatik* in 1927.[2] Five years later, Barth
markedly changed the focus and course of his dogmatics. Having
gone to Bonn, his attention to ethics, begun at Münster, was
sustained "in detail and following the particular course on
which he had embarked".[3] These two semesters on ethics in
Münster were published only after Barth's death in 1968, in
distinction to his dogmatics. They were repeated in Bonn.
The *Christliche Dogmatik* was abandoned rather than revised and
superceded by the monumental *Kirchliche Dogmatik* (1932 to 1967).
The ethics, as embodied in the *CD* (II/2, III/4, IV/3:2) remains unfinished. The first *systematic* exposition remained
unpublished, therefore, until five years after Barth's death
(vol. I reviewed here) and again until ten years after his
death (vol. II reviewed here). As things turned out, *Dei
providentia et hominum confusione* (to use a favourite phrase
of Barth's, which denotes the purposeful contingency characteristic of human existence *in regno gratiae*), Barth's insistence upon ethics as intrinsic to dogmatics resulted in an
unfinished work. The unfinished *Dogmatics* necessarily included an incomplete account of theological ethics. And why not?
The 'unfinished' is a reminder that most theological *Summa*
and also important mediaeval cathedrals remained behind, as
Barth was to put it.[4] He reminded us that death interrupted
Mozart's work on the Requiem in the middle of the *Lacrimosa*,
and that Schubert's 'Unfinished' symphony is widely celebrated.
Both in Holy Scripture and in *CD* II/2, perfection is appropriately reserved for God, and thus not to be striven for or
imitated in a human work.

This incomplete state, of course, underlines the importance of the publication of these two volumes which make avail-

able "the only complete formulation of the doctrine of sanctification, including the elaboration of specific questions".
They also exhibit "the first developed doctrinal configuration
of Karl Barth's which we possess" (I, viiif.). One must be
grateful to the editor for his decision to undertake this project and be impressed with the care and competence with which
he has prepared this edition. A word of thanks and praise is
due also to the publisher for a text which is a delight to
read.

The text is based upon two previous documents. The first
is the typescript of Barth's original manuscript, prepared for
the lectures as given in course. The manuscript is no longer
extant. The typescript, however, was prepared by Charlotte
von Kirschbaum, on the basis of the manuscript and as corrected
by dictation, thus, making the lectures ready for delivery.
This typescript is the existing original. There is, then, a
second document, a copy of the original which Barth's friend,
Rudolf Pestalozzi, arranged for and allowed to be hectographed
and distributed by the World Student Christian Federation in
Geneva. The copy consists of two monographs, dated 1929, and
comprises *Ethics I*, 254 pages, and *Ethics II*, 301 pages (I,
ix).

Barth, the perfectionist, (*CD* II/1 notwithstanding) had
the habit of going over material for a given lecture on a
given day. He added explanations or amplifications in the
margins, some in ink and some in pencil. This enlargement of
the original is the merit of the Pestalozzi hectograph, for it
enables the reader to 'hear' the lectures as delivered at
Münster and two years later in Bonn. This amended original is
identified by the editor of the published volumes as Text A.
There are other emandations, similarly in the margins, but
entered later as afterthoughts, which did not get into the
Pestalozzi hectograph of 1929. The conjecture that suggests

10

itself is that since Barth repeated the lectures in Bonn during the Summer and Winter terms of 1930-1931, he took this occasion to make further alterations in the original typescript, prepared by Charlotte von Kirschbaum. Some confirmation of this conjecture is supplied by the lecture notes of students who actually heard the lectures, notably Helmut Traub and Helmut Gollwitzer. The published edition thus rests upon Text B, which is really Text A (the Pestalozzi hectograph), plus the emandations added in Bonn. These emendations are indicated in the published text in brackets above the line. When words or phrases have had to be altered slightly for the sake of smooth reading, the change from Text A has been noted by the editor at the bottom of the page. These changes are, of course, inconsequential (I, ix.).

As things turned out, Barth's decision not to publish the Münster and Bonn lectures has provided the best reason for publishing them posthumously. In my opinion none of the projected volumes in the Complete Edition will prove to be as self-authenticating as the two volumes on ethics before us. Although what is yet to come may amplify, illuminate, and even entertain, none of the volumes to come will exhibit the focus, direction, scope, and development of Barth's thought as does this compendium of Barth's account of theological ethics. These 939 pages present both a précis of the conceptuality, content, and concreteness of ethics, theologically considered, and an exhilarating portrayal of the precision of the thematic line and the surprising subtlety is conspicuously evident in the rise of interrogative sentences now to expresss this nuance, now that, now what is included, now what is excluded, as the line of conceptual analysis unfolds. It is noteworthy that in the general ethics and in the special ethics as explicated in *CD* II/2 and III/4, the interrogative has virtually given place to the indicative, but in Münster and Bonn, the

theological exploration of ethics was marked by a tentative
nature appropriate to the exploration of themes, departing
from the traditional ways of thinking about ethics, a change
of which the author was neither unaware nor proud.

The courage and integrity of this experimentation are
attested to by both Barth's own reasons for denying publication to these early forays and by the testimony, which their
eventual publication supplies, that Barth knew what he was
about all along. The movement, from the first to the second
and subsequent editions of the *Römerbrief*, was paralleled by
the movement from the *Christliche Dogmatik* to the *Kirchliche
Dogmatik*. The publication of these volumes makes clear that a
similar movement was underway in the interpretation of Christian ethics. The preface to *CD* I/1 declares the rejection of
the line Schleiermacher-Ritschl-Herrmann because Barth could
no longer discover a third alternative between the grandeur
and misery of natural knowledge of God and a Protestant theology nourishing itself from its own source and standing upon
its own feet.[5]

The foreword to *Ethik* I reports that Barth confided to
Eduard Thurneysen that he could not publish the Münster lectures of 1928 because he saw in them a representation, however
preliminary, of "the doctrine of the orders of creation which
he later so passionately rejected" (vii). In retrospect, however, it appears that Barth was already on the way towards his
radical shift of priority and accent explicit in the *CD*. The
shift is now shown to be not less radical but less abrupt.
The published text before us exhibits more than echoes of an
analogia entis and a theology of experience always running
off into autonomy. We have, so that "he who runs may read"
(Hab. 2:2), a sketch *in nuce* of the structure of dogmatics,
inclusive of ethics, and of ethics when genuinely based upon
dogmatics. Without saying so, Barth simply sets about doing

what later became explicit: namely that an interpretation of
ethics, grounded in dogmatics, not only finds its warrant but
also its criterion already given to it. Such an ethic may
also correct and guard dogmatics from wandering astray, from
unfaithfulness to its own ground and norm.[6]

Two years after Barth had repeated, with emandations, the
Münster lectures in Bonn (Text B), he set about the *Church
Dogmatics*. The preface to I/1 (1932), projects five volumes
of a *Summa* on the soil of the Reformation. The *prolegomena*
are to deal with the doctrine of revelation, followed in the
second volume by the doctrine of God. Then, the plan calls
for one volume devoted to each of the doctrines of creation,
reconciliation and redemption. Then follows the pertinent
projection for a theological ethic. The focus, the context,
and the structure of ethics are declared to be the doctrine of
the command of God; ethics as integral to dogmatics; and, the
preview of the argument to be unfolded. ". . .the concept of
the command of God in general will be treated at the close of
the doctrine of God. The command of God from the standpoint
of *order* will then be discussed at the close of the doctrine
of creation, from the standpoint of *law* at the close of the
doctrine of reconciliation, and from the standpoint of *promise*
at the close of the doctrine of redemption".[7]

Events did not turn out that way. There is more about
order in the Münster-Bonn lectures than in *CD* III/4, where
freedom is the focus of the argument. Even in *Ethik* I, the
emphasis on *order* is carefully circumscribed. There is more
about *law* in these lectures, again carefully circumscribed
than in *CD* IV/3:2, where the accent is upon *calling* to speci-
fically Christian action (cf. *CD* IV/4). This, the last of the
Dogmatics volumes from Barth's own pen and oversight, is fragmentary. Once again, the importance of the belated publication of the early lectures is highlighted by the outline of

the conceptuality which includes the ethics of redemption, as
Barth first tried his hand at what would have become *CD* volume
V.

Under the thematic line: *The Word of God as the Command
of the Creator, the Reconciler, the Redeemer*, the schematism
looks like this:

	Creator	Reconciler	Redeemer
Means: (Perspective)	Life	Law	Promise
Reveals itself as: (Knowledge)	Calling	Authority	Conscience
Requires: (Content)	Order	Humility	Thankfulness
Bestows: (Fulfillment)	Faith	Love	Hope

This schematism was rearranged and dispersed, as the
Münster-Bonn lectures were elaborated and extended in the *CD*.
These elaborations were chiefly exegetical and concerned concrete human conditions and interrelationships. The general
ethics of *CD* II/2 is anticipated in the introduction and chapter one of *Ethik* I, whereas the special ethics (begun in *CD*
III/4 and continued in IV/3:2 and IV/4, are anticipated in
Ethik I, chapter 2, and *Ethik* II, chapters 3 and 4. It should
also be noted that the instructive section on church and state
in *Ethik* II, pages 324ff, as it appears in Text B, is accompanied by the original version of Text A, given in the appen-
dix (p. 457ff.).

The argument of these two volumes is that the command of
God is God's sovereign claim upon human kind, response to
which is the source and meaning of responsible action. The
claim of God is God's freely-given way of being related to
everything that is not God, in particular to human beings whom

he has determined for companionship with himself. As claim,
authority and freedom, sovereignty and un-coerced acceptance
are given with a divinely initiated action toward human kind
and a divinely-enabled acceptance of this action as at once
good and right. It is *good* in the sense that it is God's action in my favour (II, p. 2: *Gottes Gebot ist für den der
Gottes Wort hört;* God's command is for them who hear God's
Word). It is *right* in the sense that it is God whose action
towards me decides whether my action is *good* (in accord with
his action) or *bad* (a rejection in my behaviour of God's goodness towards me. II. p. 2: *Gottes Gebot ist das Ereignis, in
dem über mein Handeln, über mein Existieren das Gericht er-
gehen wird, in dem mir nicht über Gut und Böse im allgemeinen,
sondern über mein Gut--oder Bösesein Bescheid. . .gesagt
werden wird;* God's command is that event in which judgment
goes out over my actions, over my existence, that event in
which I shall be set straight not about good and bad in general but about my being good or bad. Or as I, p. 21 puts it:
in der Theologie [ist]. . .*Güte konkret jedenfalls etwas in
der Richtung des Begriffs Gottgemässheit zu verstehen;* in
theology goodness is to be understood quite concretely as that
which is in the direction of the idea of appropriateness to
God. Later, in *CD* III/4 it came out like this: "good human
action is action set free by the command of God, by his claim
and decision and judgment"(p. 5)).

There are three formative actions of God toward humankind. Each of these actions determines the focus and direction of human action as 'responsible'. The first is God's
action as creator which concentrates on life and the notion of
individual responsibility for life and the gift of life.

The second is God's action as reconciler and focusses on
the 'other' as one's fellow human being (*Mitmensch*). This
action is directed towards setting right wrongs between self

and other and between self and society, as God, in his command
operative as law, judges and restores right relations between
humankind and himself. Here Jesus Christ, as *vere deus - vere
homo*, is the paradigm of human action.

The third formative action of God is God's action as redeemer which focusses on the divine promise and assurance that
God's goodness will prevail. It is directed towards the realization of that promise in this life as it has already been
purposed for completion in the next. "In that [God] is not
only our creator, but as such. . .gives us his Word and himself in it, he announces to us already in the rationality of
his creation that he is our redeemer, that is the God who,
just as he is not subject to the preliminary character of this
world nor to death, so he desires to make us partakers of this
freedom over death, indeed, partakers of his Word and, thus,
also of his promise" (*Ethik* II, p. 371).

The concreteness of these relations and actions is best
evidenced in the perichoretic congruence of the goodness of
So-sein, Mit-sein, and Vollendet-sein (to be thus, to be together with, to be perfected) with the gift and practice of
faith and love and hope. *Per analogiam fidei*, this concreteness happens from moment to moment, as Jesus Christ is encountered in specific actions of obedience, since in God's
world, God's Word has drawn all who believe and love and hope
in him into and towards the completed story of his creation,
reconciliation, and redemption of everything that he has made.

Before Bonhoeffer, Barth knew about 'the man for others',
just as before Bonhoeffer, he set out upon a theological account of ethics from the divine command. And Barth knew better than Bonhoeffer what to do with and about conscience. He
shifts it radically from creation to redemption, and thereby
makes the conscience the focal instance of that freedom where-
with Christ has set us free in this world and the next. Cer-

tainly Bonhoeffer was for the most part faithful to what he
had learned from Barth, and thus, on the side of the angels.[8]
But what will the value-oriented, morals-and-metaphor people
in Yale and Chicago, and the characterologists at Notre Dame,
and all the process-people from the Atlantic to the Pacific do
now? They could, of course, start reading the Bible, even
though the hour is rather late. Since that is too much to hope
for, even with the stunning example of the Münster-Bonn lectures now before them, they may be left to the uninterrupted
contemplation of the tedious, irrelevant question: 'can
ethics be Christian?'

The fact remains that these two volumes document, even
for those who can read without running, a thematic concept
which might have spared many who have ventured upon the ter-
rain of ethics in the name of Jesus Christ, the problematic
flirtation with the fascination and the language of 'the land
of Canaan' (*Ethik* I, p. 30), and provisionally provided hearing aids and corrective lenses. What a liberation it is to
have heard Barth 50 years ago that Christian ethics has been
released from the debilitating bind between heteronomy and
autonomy, to be free for the open-endedness which refuses to
decide between good and bad as determinable and pragmatic
judgments and actions! The task of ethics, as Barth says, is
to call into question, not to give answers because Christian
ethics, theologically understood, is a description of sanctification. As God's act and gift, sanctification permits everything and forgives everything (Dostoevsky), in the freedom of
belonging to God in Christ, and of obeying him in and through
that concrete action which signals that Christ has set us
free.

Barth would be the last to insist that his way of thinking
theologically about ethics is the only way. *Jeder muss selber
anfangen*, he would say, everyone needs to begin on his/her own,

as once he said to me about the oncoming generation of theological students and scholars. But then, he would add, gently
and in his impish way of being utterly charming: *wer mehr
sagen will, der sehe zu, dass er nicht weniger sagt,* they who
want to say more must see to it that they do not say less.

NOTES

1. Busch, Eberhard, *Karl Barth. His life from letters and autogiographical texts,* (Philadelphia, Fortress Press, 1976), p. 126.

2. *Ibid.,* pp. 126-127, 154, 171-172.

3. *Ibid.,* pp. 181-182.

4. *CD* IV/4, p. vii.

5. *CD* I/1, p. xiii.

6. *CD* I/2, para. 22:3.

7. *CD* I/1, p. xvif; italics added.

8. As *CD* III/4, more than attests, p. 4.

2. The Theology of Schleiermacher*

Michel Despland

Even before Barth went to Göttingen in 1921 it had become clear to him that the lineage from Schleiermacher to Ritschl (who, by the way, is of Dietrich Ritschl's ancestry) to Herrmann could not be continued, certainly not by him. In 1968 Barth again stated that theologians not only must study Schleiermacher but also do so with great respect. In the quite polemical twenties such statements had a different tone; the essays "Schleiermacher's *Celebration of Christmas*", dating from 1924, and "Schleiermacher", dating from 1926, give evidence of this. They are to be found in Barth's *Theology and Church*.

This volume contains the lectures given in 1923-1924 at Göttingen. If a theological ethics cannot be appropriately founded in the general category of conscience, what consequences do arise for the interpretation of Schleiermacher and Protestant theology since from that same crucial shift of which the *Ethics* was manifestation?

> Tout a été dit. Sans doute. Si les mots n'avaient changé de sens et les sens de mots.
>
> *Jean Paulhan*

---

*Karl Barth, *Die Theologie Schleiermachers*, Dietrich Ritschl, ed., (Zürich, TVZ, 1978), pp. 480. This is volume 11 in the *Gesamtausgabe*.

"Schleiermacher is worth an in-depth historical study.
He lived through the great debate between Christianity and the
aspirations and excitements of the period between 1750-1830,
the great turning point in the history of the German spirit.
We still live in the light--or shadow--of this time. His path
remains rich in lessons, even if we think of him as a dead figure in other respects and consider only his now obsolete theological work. None of his contemporaries, with the exception
possibly of Hegel, entered into that debate in so thorough and
committed a fashion. None of the theologians of that time are
as representative of what happened then.

"But Schleiermacher is not a dead figure and his theological work is not obsolete. If there is anyone who keeps putting
in a word or two in Protestant theology today, it is Schleiermacher; he is still with us. One *studies* Paul and the Reformers,
but one *sees* with the eyes of Schleiermacher and *thinks* in his
tracks. That is true, even if we criticize or reject the most
important or all of his *theologoumena*. The presuppositions of
Schleiermacher are, consciously or unconsciously, willingly or
unwillingly, the characteristic ferment of all theological work.
I need only remind you of the fundamental proposition, so self-
evident to many that it is not even uttered, according to which
the primary object of this work, whether historically or sys-
tematically considered, is religion, piety, the Christian self-
consciousness." (1f).

With these words Karl Barth opened a course on the theology of Schleiermacher in Göttingen in November 1923. He does
not trust Schleiermacher, yet is determined to let him speak.
He plans to devote the lectures first to the pastor (examine
the sermons), then to the theologian and finally to the philosopher, following, in a reverse order, the threefold division of
theological study established in the *Brief Outline*: philosophi-

cal, historical, and practical theology.

Barth looks first at the Sunday sermons of Schleiermacher's last years. The theme of peace is singled out as
dominant. Prayer, the expression of our community with God,
is the highest manifestation of this peace. Schleiermacher,
concludes Barth, objects to any sharp opposition, to everything sudden. We then hear about the Christological sermons
on the great festivals, Christmas, Good Friday, Easter, Ascen-
sion. This time the sermons span the whole of the preacher's
lifetime and show a profound continuity in his thinking. The
Christmas sermons lead to a study of the *Christmas Eve*. This
is familiar to many, since Barth reworked these notes in 1925
to publish them as a separate essay. The sermons on Good Friday present Christ as being above the contrasts of this world.
The whole cross is translated into 'idealistic Biedermeier'
talk. The Easter sermons ignore the crisis of real death and
real life. The analogy of Christ and us underlies the whole.

The sermons on household themes illustrate his ethics.
The family and marriage is the great correlation of spirit and
nature. These sermons, with their advice concerning children,
servants and guests, show the best side of Schleiermacher.
Christianity is conceived there as a historical natural force.

Barth turns next to the theologian. (This was to keep him
occupied until the end of the semester and his 35 students
never heard of the philosopher.) He examines first the *Brief
Outline*. The rejection of speculative theology and the edifi-
cation of philosophical theology as the methodical bases of
modern science of religion are closely examined; "very spiritual and distinguished, a theology in fine evening gloves", is
the parting comment (p. 270). The historical theology lies at
the base of theological historicism: the canon is the beginning, not revelation. The Christian phenomenon is the object
of theology. Out of Kantian criticism, Schleiermacher ulti-

mately drew an agnostic, unlimited positivism   (p. 293).

   The Christian Faith is given praise for systematic unity.
Barth knew that Schleiermacher was saddened by those who read
only the introduction, the propositions borrowed from ethics.
Yet Barth believes that in these pages the soup that must be
eaten later is cooked (p. 347). Schleiermacher believed he
could avoid the choice between modern scepticism and mediaeval
objectivity (p. 346), but his 'Christian' theology, based on
religion as an element of human nature, has let in the Trojan
horse. Here Barth accepts the metaphor of Brunner. (*Die
Mystik und das Wort* was to appear in 1924 but Barth had seen
parts of manuscript (p. 7).) Aggressors penetrate into the
holy city, hidden in the feeling of absolute dependence like
in a dark capacious hollow body (p. 374-375). In this sort of
anthropocentric theology, Christianity differs from other religions only in colour and tone. There is no sickness unto
death (p. 393, 410), no sin before God, no grace of God (p.
425). The divine-human encounter has become harmless, not to
say bourgeois (p. 419).

   The final lectures deal with the *Speeches*. They do not
speak religion but about religion. They aim at persuasion.
But such parliamentary negotiations start with a white flag in
hand. The conclusion restates that Schleiermacher was the
greatest theologian of Protestantism since the Reformers, but
adds also that he brought about a degradation of Protestant
theology. It must be rebuilt at a place other than Schleiermacher's. Those who want to do better must, however, be full
of fear and trembling, since Schleiermacher did *his* thing well
(p. 461f.).

   There is much in these lectures that is memorable and
truly full of insight. Barth stresses the public ethical concerns demonstrated in these sermons. He shows Schleiermacher
preoccupied with the July Revolution, aware of the problem of

social inequality. His sort of theologian is a full citizen
(p. 74, 77, 309).[1] The sermons on marriage lead to a study of
Schleiermacher's grounds for rejection of divorce. This rejection is qualified since Schleiermacher acknowledges that
the State can allow the separation of married couples. He
does not, however, settle whether the church may remarry those
who are divorced.

The divorce issue leads Barth to an extended discussion
of the romantic ideal of love and the *Letters on Lucinde* and
the *Soliloquies* (both published in 1800). Barth notes how, in
1800, Schleiermacher expressed complete solidarity with the
moral views of Schlegel[2] at a time when a competent child of
the world like Schiller found them to be *Kitsch* (p. 218).
Against those who contrasted the mature Schleiermacher, de-
fender of hearth and home, and the youthful romantic with
tastes bordering on the pornographic, Barth stresses the unity,
the romantic ideal of love (two individuals predestined to belong to each other) which explains his early admiration for
Lucinde and his later rejection of divorce (pp. 199-228).

The pages on the still-born discipline of "Statistics"
(in the *Brief Outline*) show that Schleiermacher meant it to
be a description of the relationship between church and civil
community. Lacking any critical dimension, it was truly without future (pp. 296-297). The point is extended: what is
theology to the church if it is not critical? The world could
well do without *this* dogmatics and the church without *this*
statistics, since they were not addressing anyone (pp. 296,
316).

With the publication of these lectures, Barth's life-long
involvement with Schleiermacher can be fully evaluated.[3] One
may rightly wonder how genuinely fair Karl Barth is in his exposition. A detailed examination is now available offering a
line by line comparison of Barth's exposition of the *Christmas*

Eve and the Christmas sermons with Schleiermacher's texts. E.
H. U. Quapp's *Barth contra Schleiermacher? "Die Weihnachts-
feier" als Nagelprobe* makes a rigorous demonstration. Quapp
documents truncated citations and distorting summaries. His
verdict is severe. Schleiermacher's theology is disfigured at
the hands of Barth. The starting point in John 1:14 is never
acknowledged by the commentator.[4] Any Schleiermacher renais-
sance, Quapp adds, must take Barth seriously or it will be a
still birth.[5] The pre-Barthian view, however, according to
which Schleiermacher is a Christian theologian, says Quapp,
remains founded. I must concur. I cannot accept Barth's
judgment that in *The Christian Faith*, revelation is denied in
the introduction before it has a chance to express itself in
the body of the dogmatics (p. 421).[6] The second letter to
Lücke is not obfuscating. His reasons for not starting the exposition with the Christocentric affirmations were tactical
(pp. 358-365). F. C. Baur wrote that Schleiermacher's looks
at his ecclesiastical tradition held him back from radical
steps. Barth disagrees. Schleiermacher, he says, took every
last step he was inclined to do (p. 193). I disagree too, but
for another reason. The Christocentric tradition was the important fact. It was not a brake, but rather a positive force.

To this one must add that in 1923-1924 Barth was not yet
clear on his solution. In these lectures I find him vaguely
eloquent on his alternative. The issue may well focus on the
subject of language. Schleiermacher objects, we hear, to the
notion that there can be true words in the God relationship.
Truth cannot lie in words (p. 88). Barth speaks, with dark re-
proach, of speechlessness in Schleiermacher (e.g. p. 132, 373)
and of feeling only producing smoke and noise (p. 315, 441),[7]
but to refer to *Word* of God as if we all know what this means
is little help to those who seek an adequate understanding of
the nature of religious and theological language. (These lec-

tures indicate the beginning of an addiction to morally eloquent emphasis that underlines, or spaces out, words instead
of clarifying meanings).[8]

The publication of these lectures is welcome. They recreate the excitement of the first years of a major intellectual enterprise. They also clarify the nature of the respect
Karl Barth kept voicing for Schleiermacher: it was rather like
the praise young David must have had for Goliath. The book is
not needed by prudent disciples of any kind, but it must be
read by those who want to do better. A vast and serious challenge receives expression and shape in this encounter. Barth
may have been unfeeling and unthinking in many points, but his
struggle is real. Theology is still to be built on that much
trampled piece of ground, in spite of messy ruins accumulated
by spirited refutations and counter-refutations. Everything
has been said about the Christological starting point or focus,
just as everything has been said about the idea of religion;[9]
but everything must be reworked again and again.

One final point. In November 1923, Barth announced he
could not follow the genetic approach used earlier in his
lectures on Calvin and Zwingli in his approach to Schleiermacher. He was not prepared to insert the work of this theologian into a general historical account, because he could not
make a judgment yet of historic value about Schleiermacher.
If pushed, such judgment would be negative, he adds, and, for
the time being, he wants to let Schleiermacher speak (pp. 8-
9). -- May I venture elements for such a genetic consideration
and, possibly, a renewal of the debate?

Literary considerations may offer a helpful starting
point. A most illuminating controversy rages around the
Christmas Eve. It is also known that Schleiermacher planned
the publication of a series of 'platonic' or 'fictional' dia-
logues on Christian festivals (p. 144). The one thing to be

said about the work of 1805 is that in it Schleiermacher turns
to the genre of realistic narrative.

Hans Frei provides a good definition of this genre. In
it, individuals, as doers and sufferers of action, are set in
a clear context of external (natural and social) environment.[10]
As was pointed out elsewhere, realistic narrative is to be
contrasted with symbolic narrative, namely a story (the meaning
of which need not ineluctably be tied to the cumulative sequence of events and characters depicted".[11] The tension between the two types of narrative accounts for the sort of
autobiographical statement often found in the background of
the work of Christian theologians. Augustine, for instance,
tells of his past sin in powerful symbolic terms. "I walked
the streets of Babylon. I wallowed in its mire as if it were
made of spices and precious ointments." The next chapter has
the famous realistic vignette on the theft of the pears.[12]
The symbolic context establishes the general story of fall and
redemption, but the realistic control is there to keep the
story a 'genuine' autobiography with revealing content.[13] Now
much of the novelty of German romanticism lies in the flowering
of exclusively symbolic accounts of the life of the self.[14]
All romantics are searching for some story that will set forth
the unfolding of the universe, the life of the Absolute, the
becoming of the self, the history of nature. So we keep hearing of self-division and self-reunion, of fall and reascent.
Such symbols become all-encompassing; they are made to do
everything. They embody the logic of Being itself, provide an
epistemological theory, and give the key to introspective analysis. Some works show Schleiermacher completely bewitched by
the charms of symbolic narrative. The *Soliloquies* (1800) offer
to the readers the choicest gift a man can give; "his spirit's
intimate converse with itself". After pages of piffle about
the outer and the inner, the passive and the active, the finite

and the infinite, the transient and the eternal, we have heard
about holy freedom, individuality, and love but have learned
nothing about Schleiermacher except that he is melancholy
about the passing of the old year and has not yet found true
love.

In contrast the *Christmas Eve* (1805) marks an access to
the realistic and an end to the escape toward the symbolic.
We hear about a definite German household, defined in its
social reality (i.e. bourgeois and with realistic portrayal of
internal social relations).[15] The work is consciously fiction
and it portrays realistically possible life attitudes and theological positions. The point, the achievement, is not simply
that Schleiermacher turns to 'traditional' Christian concerns
such as the meaning of Christmas but that he has forged a new
literary genre. This genre can be labelled the realistic
theological fiction and must be perceived as the antidote to
'poetic' symbolical exuberance. The Schleiermacher who took
the pains to forge a new language is trying to give expression
to theological Christian truths in the new cultural and literary conditions.[16] His portrayal of "different conceptions of
Christianity" offered to our "comparative pondering"[17] deserves to be balanced beside Kierkegaard's portrayal, also
realistic, of the stages on life's way as path-breaking re-
newals of theological expression. These pioneers are *roman-
tiques manqués*. They are also Christian by-products of the
Romantic era. As Romantics they knew that the didactic moral-
istic, earnest style was a dead end, but as Christians, they
knew also that the self-indulgent wallowing in symbols
(whether known as speculation or poetry), did not provide the
answer.

NOTES

1. Yorick Spiegel opens his book *Theologie der bürgerlichen Gesellschaft. Sozial philosophie und Glaubenslehre bei Fr. Schleiermacher* (Munich, Kaiser Verlag, 1968) by stating that the unanswered question (unanswered because it is rarely seen) since Brunner's book, was: How could such a "mystical" theologian be so active on the political scene? (p. 9). This particular dead end in Schleiermacher's interpretation could have been avoided had Barth's, rather than Brunner's views, been printed in 1924.

2. For a recent account of the relationship between Schleiermacher and Schlegel (and a demonstration of Schleiermacher's early pull away from it), see H. Jackson Forstman, *A Romantic Triangle,* (Chico, CA, Scholars Press, 1976).

3. All of it is available now in English, except for these 1923-1924 lectures and his review of Brunner's book in "Zwischen den Zeiten", 1924, No. 8.
   1924 - "Schleiermacher's Celebration of Christmas"
   1926 - "Schleiermacher"
   1927 - "The Word in Theology from Schleiermacher to Ritschl".
        These three are to be found in *Theology and Church,* (London, SCM Press, 1962).
   1947 - "Schleiermacher" in *Protestant Theology in the 19 Century,* (Valley Forge, Judson Press, 1973).
   1968 - "Concluding unscientific postscript on Schleiermacher" in *Studies in Religion/Sciences Religieuses,* vol. 7, No. 2. Spring, 1978.

4. E. H. U. Quapp, *Barth contra Schleiermacher?* (Marburg, Karl Wenzel, 1978), pp. 40, 58-60. This small study includes also a valuable account of all interpretations of *Christmas Eve* from Schelling to E. Hirsch.

5. *Ibid.,* p. 5.

6. With the works of R. R. Niebuhr, *Schleiermacher on Christ and Religion,* and B. A. Gerrish's chapter on Schleiermacher in his *Tradition and the Modern World,* it should be

established that Schleiermacher moved from Christianity to religion and not the other way around.

7. Quapp makes a good point when he argues that irony in Schleiermacher is maieutic by always depreciating in Barth on Schleiermacher. *Ibid.*, p. 21-22.

8. In his review of Brunner's book, published right after the lectures were given, Barth is in his best form. The whole of Schleiermacher cannot be encompassed under the label "mystic". He is much richer, more complex and more sophisticated than Brunner makes him out to be. It is not enough to declare him the arch-heretic. His theology can be threatened only by an equally large achievement, but such alternative theology is not yet ready, says Barth in that review. The contrast between this review and some pages of the lectures (especially those on the *Speeches*) is striking. Clearly, there was some oral incontinence in the latter.

9. Consider Barth's statement: "At the moment when religion becomes conscious of religion, when it becomes a psychologically and historically conceivable magnitude in the world, it falls away from its inner character, from its truth, to idols." (Quoted in Rumscheidt, Martin, ed., *Footnotes to a Theology*, SR Supplements, Waterloo, Wilfrid Laurier University Press, 1974, p. 143). Can't the same be said today of faith becoming conscious of faith?

10. *The Eclipse of Biblical Narrative*, (New Haven, Yale University Press, 1974), p. 13.

11. Yu, Anthony C., "Recovering the Sense of the Story", *Journal of Religion*, Vol. 58, No. 2, April 1978, pp. 198-199.

12. *Confessions* II, 3 and 4.

13. The absense of control is illustrated by Rousseau's equally famous account of the incident over the combs of Mlle Lambercier. As a child, he is found alone in a room with combs that have been broken. The adults accuse him with absolute confidence and meet his obstinate denials with stunned disbelief. That day, according to Rousseau, he fell out of natural innocence into social existence. The story becomes a myth or archetype: appearances are against him, accusations based on appearances are made in good faith, he is innocent but cannot prove it (*Confessions: Oeuvres Complètes*, Paris NRF 1959, I, pp. 18-20) Rousseau returned to this myth to explain, excuse, his life. The myth in his works displaces the biblical narrative of the Fall--and spares him the hypothesis of a perverse heart in himself. I cannot buy his new myth be-

cause I smile, all too knowingly, at his departure from the conventions of realistic narrative. He shows no interest in telling me how in fact the combs were broken. The symbolic narrative swallows up too much of the realistic one. The symbol is too self-serving.

14. Auerbach pointed out long ago in his *Mimesis,* chap. 17, the absence of realistic fiction in German Romantic literature. He linked this to social conditions. For a further, more recent discussion, see Massey, M. C., "The Literature of Young Germany and D. F. Strauss's *Life of Jesus*", *Journal of Religion,* vol. 59, No. 3, July 1979, pp. 298ff.

15. That a family is German bourgeois is, of course, a serious liability. But at least Schleiermacher is talking about real Christianity in the real world of real people.

16. Like Brunner before me, I must allow that there are contending strains in Schleiermacher. Hans Frei has demonstrated to my satisfaction that his *Hermeneutics* are a decisive moment in the loss of biblical narrative. Schleiermacher's account of the search for understanding confirms the bent of the biblical exegete to find the meaning of the text elsewhere than in what the text does say as a realistic narrative, *Op. Cit.,* pp. 307, 318-322. Frei has a telling illustration. Schleiermacher had an articulate preference for the Gospel of John. Unlike the Synoptics, the symbolic narrative there can swallow the realistic one, and Schleiermacher could easily find the continuity of meaning in the consciousness of Jesus rather than in the historical story of interaction (p. 310-311). All I want to stress is that the *Christmas Eve* by its very literary form is a powerful reemergence of the realistic genre.

17. Schleiermacher's phrases in the preface to the second edition of the *Christmas Eve,* (quoted in Quapp, p. 101).

3. The Gospel of John*

James P. Martin

Two years after the course on Schleiermacher's
theology, Barth lectured on the gospel of John;
the full title of this course was: Interpretation of the Gospel of John. He gave the lectures in Winter-Semester of 1925-1926 at Münster and repeated them at Bonn in the summer of
1933! "As if nothing had happened."

While Barth showed what to many must seem an
extraordinary openness to the perspectives of
the history of religion 'school', his chief
concern was to establish the signigicance of
this gospel especially, in all of its pecu-
liarity, for the proclamation of the church's
witness. If Schleiermacher's preference of
this gospel over the Synoptics turned John into
a source for discerning the consciousness of
Jesus, and if Neo-Protestantism's preference
of the Synoptics over John, as exemplified by
Harnack, as sources for discerning the 'simple
gospel' are perceived as detriments to that
witness, a renewed interpretation of the gospel of John could well establish again what is
to be proclaimed in the church as *the church's*
witness.

Barth was unexpectedly obliged to provide a New Testament
course in the summer semester of 1933 because of the departure

---

*Karl Barth, *Erklärung des Johannesevangeliums,* (Kapitel
1-8), Walther Fürst, ed., (Zurich, TVZ, 1976, pp. xii, 422.
This is volume 9 in the *Gesamtausgabe.*

from Bonn of his colleague Karl Ludwig Schmidt. Barth took up
his earlier Münster lectures on the Fourth Gospel in order to
supply the need. The Münster lectures had been written out.
The editor uses this manuscript as Text A and supplies variant
readings from it to supplement the Bonn lectures which have
provided the manuscript, Text B, for this volume.

Barth corrected these earlier lectures and revised them,
dictating the results by machine for his secretary, Charlotte
von Kirschbaum. The style of these lectures reveals both a
written and an oral form but the oral predominates. The result
is that we are given a different German style than that of the
Kirchliche Dogmatik. These lectures are readable and relatively simple in style. Barth's process of revision had to
stop just when he began to lecture on the section 7:1-52.
From here on, Text A is used for the book. The change occurs
on page 336.

The historical situation in which these lectures were
given should not be overlooked. Uniformed Nazi students were
in the large student audience. The issues between the ideology of the Third Reich and the gospel as interpreted by Barth
are beginning to address each other. Barth's remark that the
Fourth Evangelist's view of the Jews was "not all a dark picture" (p. 212) and his refusal to interpret 1:17 in an anti-
Judaistic sense (p. 152f.) are examples.

Using the *lectio continua* commentary style, Barth runs
out of time at the end of Chapter 8. Because of this his book
cannot be called a complete commentary on the Fourth Gospel.
A reader, especially a *Neutestamentler*, will be disappointed
by this limitation but also sensitive to evidences that Barth
knew something about the rest of the gospel even if he did not
write it out for us. The scripture index to this volume shows
that Barth made fairly wide use of cross-references. Some
texts from Chapter 11 on are frequently cited. Barth is aware

of the central importance of the Passion Narrative for the interpretation of the whole gospel, including the parts on which
he lectures. He uses this centrality as a hermeneutical principle. He himself is conscious of the limitations of his lectures for a full understanding of the Fourth Gospel. He describes his work as "Torso: 3/7 des Evangeliums. *Anlauf* zum
Verstehen. Sphinx" (p. 398), a torso, as there are merely 3/7
of the gospel, an initial run at understanding, a Sphinx. He
thinks of it as the beginning of an exegesis, because he has
listened to the One who stands between God and us humans.

The material of these lectures varies from word by word,
verse by verse, detailed exegesis (*Einzelexegese*), especially
in the Prologue, to *thematic* discussion of sections of the
gospel, especially in Chapters 5, 6, 7, and 8. The Prologue
is given the greatest attention. In the present volume, it
occupies 151 pages. Within that space, 22 pages are assigned
to verse 14 of the Prologue. By contrast, the 71 verses of
Chapter 6 take up 30 pages and 7:1-8:11, 63 pages. These
facts indicate the result of a *lectio continua* approach which
starts from 1:1 of a biblical book and, in this case, they
show where the author wants to emphasize what is important in
his interpretation. It might appear that Barth interprets the
body of the gospel out of, and under the control of, the Prologue, but his lectures clearly and consistently show how he
seeks to explain the language of the Prologue by the language
of the rest of the gospel. The text controls all his materials,
even where a thematic approach is used.

Barth gives attention to literary structure. He analyzes
the Prologue without becoming paralyzed by analysis. He states
that Chapter 5 commences something new and provides reasons for
the statement (p. 266). Analysis extends to Greek syntax (it
hardly needs to be noted that these lectures are on the Greek
text) and Greek words. Syntax and words are analyzed and

probed for their meaning, sometimes in remarkably detailed
fashion (e.g. 1:3, 4), but where Barth discusses the meaning
of *words* he does it as a part of syntax. He does not detach
and isolate words. He listens to the whole Johannine context
as an aid to interpreting them. He refuses, for example, to
assign any meaning to *zoē* (life) in 1:4 other than the principal Christo-centric meaning it bears throughout the gospel.

In deciding the issue of the meaning of Life in 1:4,
Barth brings into his discussion the history of interpretation,
including the Fathers, Reformers and modern scholars. He includes the writers and the sources of the history of religion
school, but does not allow them to dominate. The determination of background for a Johannine expressions is not so important to Barth as the explication of the expression's
Johannine meaning (e.g. *Logos, Zoē*).

Throughout his lectures Barth debates with other inter-
preters. He functions as a church exegete, not as a member of
the modern "biblical guild" or as a fundamentalist preacher.
He listens to the history of the Church's hearing of this text,
criticizes it when he feels it is wrong, and makes his own conclusions. His partners in this conversation include (most frequently) Augustine, Calvin, Zahn, Schlatter, Coccejus, Schleiermacher, Walter Bauer, H. J. Holtzmann, and the Apostle Paul.

The introduction to the lectures (pp. 1-11) reveals a
Barth who is concerned with the hermeneutical question as he
approaches the Fourth Gospel. He turns to Augustine's *Tracta-
tus in Ioannis Evangelium* for help and repeats the question
Augustine raised in his first tractate on John 1:1-5, namely,
how is it possible for us to understand what is written, since
over us stands the judgment that the natural man cannot com-
prehend the things of the Spirit of God (I Cor. 2:14).[2] After
discussing Augustine's allegorising of the text: "Lift up
your eyes unto the hills" (Ps. 121), to mean: "Lift up your

eyes to the evangelists", Barth urges those who hear him to
do precisely this--lift up your hearts to the evangelist's
witness to God. From Augustine, says Barth, we learn that the
Johannine gospel can only be read and understood faithfully in
accordance with its subject-matter as the work of an apostle
in the 'space' defined for us by the Church, Sacrament, Canon.
The Johannine apostolic word does not witness to itself, but
to the revelation entrusted to an apostle and proceeding from
him.

There are three elements of our situation as hearers
which we must heed if we wish to understand: (1) the purpose
of the Gospel of John is to communicate faith. To study it as
such a book is to study it scientifically; to ignore this purpose is unscientific. (2) The evangelist who addresses us is
as we are, a human being whose place and time are fixed.
Therefore, we are involved in the historical problematic which
surrounds all human words. Nevertheless, the evangelist is
not apart from God a proclaimer of God and neither apart from
God can we acknowledge him as a proclaimer of God. (3) We
must "Lift up our hearts" (*sursum corda*) toward the invisible.
For our hearts to do this, they need purification and self-
control. To understand the subject-matter of the Johannine
word in the framework of its own logic and ethic requires
openness and disciplined attentiveness. (pp. 11, 12).

From these hermeneutical considerations, it might appear
that Barth has prejudged the apostolic origin of the gospel,
that is, has pre-supposed that John, the son of Zebedee, is
the author. This was the position of Barth's father, whose
lectures on the Fourth Gospel were available to Barth in manuscript, but are never cited by him. The apostolic authorship
was an important matter for Fritz Barth, but his son approaches
it in his own independent way.

For Karl Barth, the authorship question is not a mere

past-historical problem; it has to do with the matter of a
witness to revelation. The Index to these lectures reveals a
peculiar concentration on the figures of John the Evangelist
and John the Baptist. The author of the gospel, Barth notes,
is never historically named (e.g. as John, son of Zebedee),
but he is theologically described as *witness* (21:24). Barth
does not refer anywhere to 19:35 (pp. 7, 8). In the quotations
the editor provides from Barth's correspondence (pp. vii ff.),
Barth expresses himself as so taken with the Johannine *answer*
(to the question of knowledge and revelation of God) that he
has no more taste for the "Johannine *question*" (as used in
biblical scholarship). Barth's interest in the author as *witness* is evident in his exegetical discussion of the Prologue,
where he discovers how important is the author's self-
awareness as "witness". In his discussion of the difficult
problem of the "insertion" of John the Baptist into the Prologue (verses 6, 8), Barth calls attention to the relation between revelation and witness to revelation. He suggests that
the author of the gospel has concealed himself, and revealed
himself, in the witnessing function of John the Baptist. John
the Baptist's witness to one *beyond himself* is stressed (1:6-8,
15, 26, 29; 3:27). Barth goes further to wonder if John the
Baptist was not the *teacher* of the author, and that the author
learned his lesson well and in fact does nothing else throughout his gospel than what his teacher did (p. 18). The author,
like his teacher, is only *a witness to* "the lamb of God who
takes away the sin of the world". That is the theme of the
book. Christ, but never his disciple, can say, "I came as a
witness" (5:30). The result is that Barth sees the portrait
of John the Baptist as positive, not simply negative and polemical. We are reminded of Barth's life-long interest with
Grünewald's Crucifixion and its portrayal of the Baptist.

These formal considerations of the author's function as

witness and the importance of that function are subordinate, however, to Barth's exegetical concentration on the *material* character of the Johannine witness. "John" witnesses to Jesus Christ. A characteristic example is more useful to exemplify this concentration than general statements about it. On v. 2 of the Prologue, Barth discusses the exegetical problem of the *houtos* which commences the verse, debates with Zahn on it, and concludes with Schlatter that the demonstrative does not refer backward to *logos* but forward and indicates the same *houtos* as verse 15. Although the actual name of Jesus is not used, says Barth, these demonstratives clearly mean Jesus. The whole Prologue, in all its development is wholly about Jesus Christ. For the author, Jesus is the Logos, Jesus is the Life, Jesus is the Light shining in darkness. Barth adduces Zahn and Schlatter in support, and also Eduard Thurneysen.[1]

Throughout the lectures, this focus on Jesus Christ is everywhere evident. Exegetically, it is impressive and theologically it is fascinating to observe how carefully Barth listens to the witness of the text. The texts do not witness primarily to the 'religious experience' of the author or of the Johannine church, but to the one whose story and word is the reality which gives experience and calls into being a community of believers. Certainly the Barthian interest in revelation and Word of God is present and, if revelation is problematical, Word is surely a pivotal Johanning term, the use and meaning of which require a term such as revelation to describe its function and effect.

The book must be read to appreciate Barth as an exegete. He takes seriously the special language of the texts and does not reduce them all to a monotonous Christological formula. He knows the monotony, but does not succumb to it. His personalism allows him freedom to let the varieties of text bear their witness to Jesus Christ, not to an idea, ideology or doctrine.

He also listens to the text in terms of his own context. Thus,
in considering the witness of the Cana sign (2:1-11) to Christ,
Barth takes time to discuss the 'alcohol question' which some
raise in terms of Jesus' making wine.

He does not develop the eschatology of the Fourth Gospel
as a *locus*, but as a language in the service of Christ. Although aware of the double eschatology in the gospel, he does
not isolate it as a thing in itself to be discussed in isola-
tion, but in its function as witness. This seems to present a
sort of realized eschatology, but not as a solution to a problem of time. Rather, the end is present for us in Christ.
The *Eschatos* is more important in the Johannine text than an
eschaton.

He argues that the arrival of grace and truth in Jesus
Christ does not mean the denigration of the law given through
Moses (1:17) nor a disqualification of what God gave through
Moses. In the Fourth Gospel Moses and his law stand well in
their place. Barth stresses the action of God in *giving* what
Moses received. The text (1:17) contains no *men. . .de* or
alla, no adversative. There is no need to engage in anti-
Jewish polemics in order to support the witness to Jesus Christ.
Barth usually uses the witness of Moses, Abraham and Isaiah
positively, perhaps almost self-evidently, without entering
into the actual polemics within the Johannine Church as understood by recent New Testament scholarship. Now and then a reminder to the *Römerbrief* appears, as in the statement of 1:51
that the reign of the Messiah comes vertically from above
(*senkrecht von oben*) or it does not come at all (p. 187). Yet
in commenting on 4:22 ("salvation is from the Jews"), Barth
stresses that the reality of 'the Jews' is *where* the Lord became flesh.

Throughout the lectures, it is possible to discuss Barth's
appreciation for *grace*. This is not argued explicitly in so

many words, but in the ways in which he will in any given text
emphasize the Divine initiative, willingness and action. On
the story of the woman of Samaria, stress is put on Jesus'
willingness to *give* her the living water, just as God's
giving the law to Moses was highlighted. In Chapter 5, Jesus'
willingness to heal is accented and related to the hour of
true worship (4:23) which now, in Chapter 5, appears as the
hour of healing, to make alive. In Chapter 6, Jesus gives
true food which abides to eternal life. Barth also emphasizes
the Father's giving authority to the Son to have life in himself as the ground for the Son's power to make alive   (5:26
and context).

Barth is aware of the dark side of the Johannine witness.
He comments that Chapter 5 is "another world" in comparison
with the world of 4:46ff (p. 271). He is astonished, but not
daunted, by the genuine chaos in Chapter 7 with its voices
from all sides, and appreciates the relative calm of Chapter
8 after the confusion of Chapter 7. He interprets the theme
of Chapter 7 to be the disturbance Jesus brings to Jerusalem
by his word. He quotes Calvin's observation that different
times are represented in Chapter 7 and that it does not present a continuous historical narrative. But, although similar
comments could be cited to show Barth's awareness of the
Johannine style, he does not resort to literary chronological
rearrangement to change the style. He focuses everything on
the word of Jesus and on faith in Jesus. The Johannine view
of judgment is so focussed by Barth. "Those who have done
good" and "those who have done evil" (5:29) Barth explains as
customary eschatological speech, which in the Johannine context
refers to believers and unbelievers. Resurrection to judgment
is resurrection to the *awareness* of their unbelief. Judgment
is, therefore, thoroughly Christocentric.

In his analysis and thematic discussion of Chapter 6,

Barth is puzzled by the second sign. Why is it needed? How is it related to what follows, where, unlike the first sign, it is not explicitely referred to again. He concludes that the second sign, centered on the "It is I, be not afraid" is related to the theme of unbelief which runs throughout the chapter and is focussed on the circle of disciples (verses 60-71) who were the lone recipients of the second sign.

An extended discussion on the Johannine understanding of the Eucharist is provided, with some inclusion of the Luther-Zwingli debate on 6:63. John, according to Barth *presupposes* an institution of the Eucharist but does not himself provide one. Neither does John provide a doctrine of the Eucharist. The Johannine text is, however, a complete equivalent for a history or a doctrine of the Eucharist. It has "no special content over against the proclamation of the Word and the doctrine of the Word" (p. 316). Barth totally ignores the relation of 13:1-30 to the Johannine eucharistic practice. The foot-washing episode is not even cross-referenced. Here the history of doctrine has prevailed over exegetical endeavour. The neglect of the resurrection promises in Chapter 6, verses 39, 40, 44, may have contributed to the traditional conclusions concerning the Eucharist. No explanation is offered as to why there should be a eucharistic practice at all in the Johannine church given the obvious proclivity of the author for the Word.

It is at this point that the differences between Barth's time and interests and those of a later time with other interests in the Johannine gospel become most apparent. We think especially of recent research into the history and character of the Johannine church vis-à-vis its contemporary Judaism. But one cannot expect Barth to say the final word which will end all further research into this gospel. Nevertheless, we must be impressed with his faithfulness to the central subject of the Johannine witness.

These lectures, published as part of the project of a
Complete Edition of Barth's works are to be welcomed in terms
of the project. These lectures will be evaluated by different
people for different purposes. To pose the question: "are
they a contribution to literature on the Fourth Gospel or to
literature on Karl Barth?" is to pose a false alternative.
First of all, they are a contribution to a study of Barth's
thought. They are valuable for this purpose, coming as they
do chronologically after the *Romerbrief* and *I Corinthians* and
before the *Church Dogmatics.* These lectures will help correct
some false conclusions still prevailing from opponents of his
letter to the Romans. Barth is a theological exegete, not a
dogmatic one. His hermeneutical concerns are very much ours
today. There is probably more agreement by New Testament
scholars today than some of them would dare to admit. This is
as it should be, because Barth disliked those who were concerned with *him* rather than with the questions he was concerned
with.

Compared with Romans, these lectures on John are less
dominated by Kierkegaard, and more concerned with historical
exposition without getting lost in the past. Barth's exposition reminds one of Calvin. He combines exegetical skill with
theological seriousness and an almost intuitive sense of the
subject-matter. A theological commentary moves in the direction of proclamation without losing its anchor in a critical
reading of the 'origins' of the text, and without becoming a
dated sermon, testifying more to the contemporary concerns of
the 1920's and 1930's instead of the one who is Lord of both
origins and the 1930's--and 1980's. Theological interpretation
lies in the center of the dynamics of the unceasing movement
of *explicatio, meditatio,* and *applicatio:* it always speaks of
Jesus Christ who was, is, and will be. It takes seriously the

scientific responsibility of accepting the objectivity of the invitation to faith.

The difference between Barth and some of his contemporaries may be illustrated by his discussion of the words of Jesus to the woman of Samaria concerning the coming hour of true worship (4:21ff). He argues that the conversation on the subject of the five husbands exposes the relativities of *Religionsgeschichte*. The Father's act of seeking true worshippers through Jesus' act of giving the living water (the *Spirit*, 7:38) is the *end* of the history of religions. The Trinity, says Barth here, is the answer to the problem of the relativity of the history of religions. We perceive here some lines of thought developed into the treatment of the subjects of the Trinity and religion in the *Church Dogmatics*. We also see why he could use the materials from the history of religions-school without being too impressed by them.

In the perspective of the history of the interpretation of the Fourth Gospel, Bultmann's massive commentary will overshadow Barth's lectures. A comparison of the two would be useful but lies beyond our scope. The contrasts are striking: one is the work of a major critical New Testament scholar, the other the product of a giant among theologians. The *Neutestamentler* knows what Barth "left out" of his lectures, but he also knows how much Bultmann "put in" to the Johannine gospel. While Barth's lectures are not a major contribution to Johannine literature, any teacher of the Gospel will learn much from his faithful listening to the Johannine witness. Hermeneutically he is on the right track.

NOTE

1. Thurneysen, Eduard, "Der Prolog zum Johannesevangelium", in *Zwischen den Zeiten*, vol. 3, (1925), pp. 12-37.

4:   Church Dogmatics IV/4*

Charles C. Dickinson

This volume contains what Barth thought would
be his last lectures. As things turned out,
he 'succeeded' himself for one semester, in the
winter of 1961, in which he delivered his 'introduction': *Einleitung in die evangelische
Theologie*. Many of us at Basel then expected
Barth to continue his work on the "Our Father",
to conclude perhaps in that semester what he
had begun in semesters before. But we were introduced to theology, instead. How appropriate!
Entitled 'The Christian Life', this volume
speaks directly to the social and political dimension of life. As dogmatics, these lectures
are both instruction and injunction concerning
the way our history is to be made appropriate
to the history of Jesus Christ in our midst.
And the fundamental character of that appropriateness is our human calling for God. (*Rufe
mich an*, translated into *Call for God*, was the
title of Barth's last volume of sermons).

Thus, as it began, this section concludes with
a view to ethics.

Karl Barth's *Church Dogmatics* remains incomplete. Volume
V: "The Doctrine of Redemption" was never written. Volume IV:
"The Doctrine of Reconciliation" was not finished. Volume III:
"The Doctrine of Creation" and Volume IV end with a part-

---

*Karl Barth, *Das christliche Leben: Die Kirchliche Dog-
matik IV/4 Fragmente aus dem Nachlass, Vorlesungen 1959-1961*,
Hans-Anton Drewes and Eberhard Jüngel, eds., (Zürich, TVZ,
1976), pp. XX, 536. This is volume 7 in the *Gesamtausgabe*.

volume of ethics, viz. Volume IV/4 containing chapter 17, 'The
Command of God the Reconciler'. This chapter was to contain
an introductory section, numbered paragraph 74, a section on
baptism as 'the *foundation* of Christian life', numbered paragraph 75, an explication of the Lord's Prayer as a *presenta-
tion* of the Christian life, numbered paragraphs 76-78, and one
more concluding section on the Lord's Supper as the *renewal*
of Christian life. The fragment on baptism was published sep-
arately (1967 in German, 1969 in English). The present volume
contains an editor's introduction, then paragraph 74, the thesis of paragraph 75 and paragraphs 76, 77, and 78 on the open-
ing address and the first two petitions of the Lord's Prayer.
The rest was never written. Together, the two published fragments make up less than half of the planned *CD* IV/4.

The title of this volume, "The Christian Life", which
also figures in the title of Barth's published fragment on
baptism, is an explicit echo of Calvin's *Institutio* III/6:
"On the Life of the Christian". As the key-term of *CD* III/4
("The Command of God the Creator") was *freedom*, so the key-
term originally selected by Barth for IV/4 was *Treue*, faithfulness or loyalty or fidelity. But, as Barth's letters indicate,
he subsequently concluded that the rubric should be *Anrufung
Gottes*, invocation of God, calling upon God, or simply call
for God.[1] The allusion is clearly to Psalm 50:15. For water-
baptism is not a "sacrament" but a *petition* for the Holy Spirit
as the foundation of Christian life; the petitions of the Lord
Lord's Prayer represent the Christian life, and the Lord's
Supper is not a "sacrament" but is the *thanksgiving*, the "eucharist", which renews the Christian life.

Following this schematic summary of the volume, we present four detailed notes on contents and four critical comments.

1: *The Knowledge of God*. Paragraph 77 comments on the
petition "Hallowed be your name". Its second subsection is

entitled "The Known and the Unknown God". In it Barth states "it must not be *forgotten* that God's being known in the world must, given the centre of Christian faith, be much *more interesting* and much *more important* to us, than the fact that he is also unknown to it" (p. 207). Yet, one of the most interesting sections of the book is Barth's own description of the four forms of God's being unknown in the world. Least harmful is "theoretical atheism", somewhat harmful is "religion", by which Barth here means primarily idolatry. More harmful yet is what Barth interestingly calls the "nostrification of God", the notion that we have God, *habemus Deum*, that because "God is with us", therefore everything we do infallibly becomes "the will of God". (Compare the slogan of the First Crusade: *Deus vult*, God wills it.) But most harmful of all is a--or the--*practical* result of the foregoing: the misjudment or misunderstanding (*Verkennung*) of our fellow-humans, the notion that, because our fellow-humans are means only and not ends in themselves, our attitude towards them is, therefore, a matter of total indifference, with the result that *homo homini lupus*. --One need not look very far in order to find more than one example of these latter three forms, "religion", nostrification of God, reification of the fellow-human, combined into one single, virulent exemplar!

2: *The Name of God.* The third subsection of paragraph 77 is called "Hallowed be your name". Barth's main point here is that, although we may and must do our little part to hallow or sanctify God's name, only *God alone* can truly and fully hallow and sanctify his own name as it really should and must be (and already is in itself, but not yet in the world). Thus, this petition is in fact an *eschatological* petition (p. 286).

3: *The Kingdom of God.* In commenting on the petition "Your kingdom come", Barth (and the editors) provide a brief history of the interpretation of the concept of "the kingdom

of God" from Origen to Fritz Buri (pp. 411-422): whether,
platonizingly, as a state of the soul, of the church (or as
the Church itself: Augustine), of "the Christian world", or
of all humanity. All of these, except the Blumhardts' concept,
objects Barth, are immanent, intra-worldly, uneschatological
interpretations and, thus, do not do justice to the "eschatological" and indeed apocalyptic character of the kingdom of
God as envisioned in Deutero and Trito Isaiah and the New Testament. But Barth himself, whether or not he realizes the
mythological character of such biblical eschatological and
apocalyptic conceptions, in fact "demythologizes" them to the
effect that God comes to us eschatologically (p. 426) "new
every morning" (Lam. 3:23). The kingdom of God is God himself,
who again and again frees and summons people to their own eschatological existence in the present, to a being in human
righteousness and to works of human righteousness (p. 422), so
that it, the *novum* for which Christians pray: your kingdom
come!, is already "the *future* in the present, the *beyond* in
the here, the *last* is the first with which they have to do"
(p. 427). Barth later identifies God's kingdom with Christ
himself and with Christ's kingdom (pp. 432-35) and proceeds to
describe how the New Testament community turned 180 degrees
from looking back at the earthly Jesus to looking forward for
the coming heavenly Christ in their search for the kingdom of
God, while not forgetting the earthly Jesus (pp. 435-443).
But the significance of the kingdom of God remains, for Barth
God's eschatological coming-anew-every-day and the Christians'
new-every-day eschatological existence, except that now this
eschatological existence is characterized by a very christological concentration.

4: *The Method of Theological Ethics.* Under discussion
is Barth's final volume of ethics. For the theologian, one of
the most interesting features of the book must be Barth's re-

newed discussion of his ethical *method* ("meta-ethics"). For
those familiar with his earlier ethical sections in the
Church Dogmatics, with his essay "Gospel and Law", and others,
there is little new here. Just as in *CD* III/4 Barth tried to
steer between Emil Brunner's "orders of creation" (natural law
as the complement of natural theology) and Søe's situation
ethics by taking a leaf from Dietrich Bonhoeffer's *Ethics* and
speaking of realms of human life which "are not things like
laws, prescriptions, imperatives", but are "spheres in which
God commands and in which man is obedient or disobedient"[2],
so here again Barth tries to steer between legalism and situation ethics, between sheer static "being" and sheer anarchic,
punctiliar "act".[3] Barth completes his meta-ethics in the
section entitled "The Priority of the Word of God" (especially
pp. 294-308), where he details how God's Word must have not
the *total*, but indeed the *primary* validity in the Christians'
life: among all the demands laid upon us, and in all the decisions and choices we make among various possible courses of
action, the Word of God must be the *guiding principle*.

    5. *The Command of God.* In light of recent developments
in theology and culture, it must be said that one of the most
questionable (albeit central) aspects of Barth's ethics is his
characterization of Christian ethics as "the command of God".
My question to Barth here is this: how is "command" different
from "law"? (Huldrych Zwingli and Dean Eenigenburg talk of
"the will" of God, but it comes to the same thing.) Is "law"
written, but a "command" not?[4] And even if "Torah" originally
meant not "Law" but "instruction", it certainly came to mean
"Law" by and to the prophets who interpreted the Exile as
God's punishment, or "chastisement" (Isaiah 53:5), for Israel's
disobedience to God's Torah in general, culminating in Israel's
unfaithfulness to God,[5] not to mention the legalistic interpretation by the Pharisees and Rabbis of "Judaism".[6] Indeed,

Barth cites Matt. 5:17f (p. 44; these verses are often considered Matthew's addition) to affirm that Jesus brought a
nova lex (*sic*) which does not abolish but fulfills the law of
Moses; Barth cites, approvingly and literalistically, the "law
of Christ" of Galatians 6:2, the "new commandment" of John 13:
34 and I John 2:8, Paul's self-description as *énnomos Christoû*
of I Corinthians 9:21, Matthew 7:24ff, and Romans 1:5 on the
"obedience of faith" (Barth's emphasis). Now, Barth indeed
polemicizes against the static, formalistic "abstract legalism"
of non-Christian religions and of Christianity, too (pp. 54ff).
But why is a "dynamic" (p. 49), substantial, concrete "command",
even if it is called "Jesus Christ" (paragraph 74, subsection
2 *passim*), any less potentially whimsical, arbitrary, despotic,
tyrannical, "heteronomous" (even if it is called "theonomy"),
than a static, formalistic, abstract "law"? Why is the "rule
of man" necessarily better than the "rule of law", even if
that "man" be identified with "God"? ("Islam", I recall, means
absolute "submission" to the will of a very arbitrary and
"dynamic" God.)--Here, of course, enters the whole issue of
"law and gospel". According to a certain Lutheran *ordo
salutis* of "law, then gospel", the harsh, stern, judgmental,
"just" or "righteous" God of the Old Testament gave Israel a
law containing no whit of grace (Law as the harsh "pedagogue
unto Christ", Gal. 3:24) until a somehow mellowed God of mercy,
goodness, and forgiveness sent his son "Christ the end of the
Law" (Rom. 10:4) to redeem and accept all believers as justified by grace through faith apart from the works of the Law
(Eph. 2:5, 8f). To this Barth opposed his own *ordo salutis*
of "gospel and law"[7] according to which, in both the Old and
the New Testaments, gospel and law ("command") are simply the
obverse and reverse of one and the same grace of God. But
neither order, it would seem, is quite biblical. For: (a)
According to the Old Testament writers, both Exodus *and* Sinai

(Torah), as well as the Conquest and perhaps even the Wilderness, are all forms of the one grace in which God elected Israel. But what is a form of grace to an ancient Near Eastern nomadic people, for example divine Law of "command", is not necessarily thereby a form of grace to 20 century Western people. (b) According to Paul, Galatians 3, the period of the Law from Moses to Christ was simply an *interlude* between two periods of promise and faith, that is between the period of Abraham and the period of Christ. Thus, indeed, "Christ is the *telos*", the culmination *and* the end, "of the Law" (Rom. 10:4). Consequently, what we could propose *sub specie biblica et Paulina*, is neither the Lutheran nor the Barthian *ordo salutis*, but rather the one grace of the one gracious God, which "at sundry times and in various ways" (Heb. 1:1) took the form of Promise, Exodus, Sinai (Torah), Wilderness, Conquest, Monarchy, Temple, Prophets, Exile, Restoration, etc., but which in Christ has just as decisively put an end to a number of them, including Law ("command") *as Law* (Rom. 10:4), in favour of the renewed Promise, faith, and freedom *under* God (Gal. 5:1, 13) of the mature, "come-of-age" sons and daughters of God (Gal. 4:1-7; Rom. 8:14-17) and not "immature. . .infants" (p. 126).

6. *Freedom as Obedience*. Corresponding to Barth's notion of God's "command" is his Kantianizing interpretation of our only possible "freedom" (not just Christian, but any possible human freedom whatsoever) as perfect "obedience" to the command of God. It is "Kantianizing" because, just as for Kant our sole possible freedom consists in absolute obedience to the Categorial Imperative, so for Barth our sole possible freedom is "the freedom of *obedience*" (p. 423, Barth's emphasis), and "command and obedience" are the sole possible nexus of the relationship of God and us (p. 43).

7. *Christian Immaturity*. Of a piece with the foregoing

is Barth's insistence that those who call God "Father" can
meet him only as *immature infants*. "Those who through God's
grace have the freedom to call on God as their Father, the
grace being that Jesus Christ became and is their brother, will
by making use of this freedom meet God on no occasion other
than as untrained, unexperienced, incapable persons *not of age,*
and hence in this sense, as children, as *infants* utterly unpre-
pared for that meeting" (p. 126, Barth's emphases). One of the
most fascinating and sophisticated, yet also exasperating subsections of this volume is the one entitled "The Lordless
Powers" (pp. 363-399), those "principalities and powers", in
Paul's language, who gain control of those who think that, by
freeing themselves from God, they will be free indeed. Barth's
analysis is *fascinating* in its sophisticated identification
"*man's own. . .powers*" (p. 366, Barth's emphasis) as the very
entities which, once we have emancipated ourselves from God,
also emancipate themselves from us, their whilom possessors,
and enthrone themselves *over* us as "thrones, dominions, principalities, authorities (cf. Col. 1:16). As such powers today
Barth identifies the state ("Leviathan" of Rev. 13), Mammon,
various ideologies and "isms", technology, fashion, sports,
amusements, traffic and travel.

But Barth's analysis is also exasperating, not in itself
but in the use to which he puts it: in his use of these "Lordless powers" as terrible examples of what happens to us when
we attempt to progress the status of "immature infants", which
Barth thinks the gospel of God's fatherhood requires us to be
and to remain (as argued in subsections 1 and 2 of Paragraph
76), a use much like that of parents of spooks and goblins to
terrify their children into obedience. Now indeed, the biblical injunction to become "childlike" (e.g. Matt. 18:3f) is well
made against all "superlative apostles" (2 Cor. 11:5) and other
arrogant, authoritarian, and imperialistic Christians. But

Barth's injunction to be "childish" and indeed "infantile",
especially when stated so undialectically, just as easily and
fatally falls into the hands of just such authoritarian Christians who would and do use it to keep other Christians from a
Christian *sapere ande!*, from making free, unfettered, and autonomous use of their own independent reason. Such injunction
flies directly into the face of such passages as Gal. 4:1-7,
Rom. 8:14-17, and Heb. 5:12-14, 6:1, and is absolutely fatal
to any attempt, pastoral or otherwise, to nurture or even
sanction a Christian or any other form of what is absolutely
essential to healthy life, namely maturity. For these reasons,
I must, with Friedrich Gogarten[8] eschew the word "children" in
favour of "mature sons and daughters" of God, as that which
Christians are called and should strive to be.[9]

8. God as *"Benevolent Despot"*. Finally, I note two characteristics of "Barth's" God, as presented here and throughout
the *CD*. (a) Corresponding to his characterization of Christians as "immature infants" is his markedly paternalistic conception of God. Perhaps something of the sort was inevitable
in the context of Barth's interpretation of the phrase "Our
Father" for which, unfortunately, Barth did not have available
the crucial essay *Abba* by Joachim Jeremias.[10] At all events,
Barth's treatment of God as "Father" (pp. 75-110) reminds us
once again, as do the articles on *pater* and *huios* in Kittel's
Theological Wordbook, that the New Testament appelation of God
as "Father" and of Jesus Christ as his "Son" is and can, like
all significant language about God, only be a *metaphor* or
model: at best analogical, at worst mythological.[11] (b)
Closely related to Barth's "paternalistic" conception of God
is his portrayal of God as doing everything he does *ultimately*
for the sake, not of the creature, but of *his own glory*. Such
a conception is, of course, not new. In Protestant theology,
its seed is in Zwingli, its flower in Bucer and Calvin. "Zwing-

li commonly made the good of the creature the controlling motive in all divine activity; but in his work, *On Providence*. . .
he spoke [following Augustine] of election as a manifestation
of the divine mercy, and of reprobation as a manifestation of
divine justice [*Opera*, 1828ff., IV, 115]. By Bucer this was
made controlling, and the motive of predestination was represented, not as the good of the creature, but as the exhibition
of the glory of God".[12] McGiffert then goes on to show how
Bucer's ideas influenced Calvin. The presence of this idea in
Barth is unmistakable, here as elsewhere: "He is, namely, the
God who has set out and again and again sets out to go, in the
whole mystery of his godhead, out of his aseity (blossen Gott-
heit) and to enter into the human world which he created,
which without him would be lost, which hs is to save and to
make new, all this in order to confirm his *lordship* over it,
which human presumption, folly and deceit, together with their
subsequent misery had put into question: *to establish his
honour* precisely by giving himself over to the world, for the
world, for its salvation" (p. 19: my emphases). Here again,
as with Anselm, the "honour of God" is God's own "ultimate
concern". Indeed, whereas for Bucer God's exhibitory *predestination* is the chief means, for Barth God's exhibition and
exercise of his divine *love* is the chief means of God's self-
glorification. Though the means may differ, the end remains
the same. All this is made most explicit in the longest section of the volume, 166 pages: "Zeal for the Honour of God"
on the petition "Hallowed be your name", and especially the
first sub-section of this Paragraph 77: "The Great Passion"
which is, of course, precisely that "zeal for the honour of
God".

A final word: "Modernism may be either conservative or
revolutionary. It is conservative where the subordination of
the old to the new saves the old from destruction. . . It is

revolutionary where the subordination takes the form of a
nullification of the old. . . .The conservative species of
modernism occurs among religions"[13] and not least, I might
add, in the theology of Karl Barth. Or, to change the metaphor, Karl Barth has fashioned *new* wineskins, the better to
preserve *old* wine. Yet, from old wine to vinegar is but a
short step indeed.

54

NOTES

1. *Call for God* became the title in English of Barth's
last volume of sermons to be published by him.

2. Busch, Eberhard, *Karl Barth*, p. 376.

3. See Bonhoeffer, Dietrich, *Act and Being*, as well as
James Gustafsen's way between Paul Ramsey's rules and norms
and Paul Lehmann's situation ethics.

4. In the military service of the United States, a verbal "command" or "order" is valid for 24 hours, a written one
until recinded.

5. See Rad, Gerhard von, *Old Testament Theology*, vol.
II; Ricoeur, Paul, *The Symbolism of Evil*, Chapter II, "Sin".

6. Ricoeur, *ibid.*, Chapter III, "Guilt".

7. The German edition of *Evangelium und Gesetz* was first
published in 1935; the English translation appeared in 1959.

8. *Der Mensch zwischen Gott und Welt*, (Stuttgart, Friedrich Vorwerk Verlag, 1956), pp. 329-331.

9. See Tillich, Paul, *Systematic Theology*, vol. I,
(Chicago, The University of Chicago Press, 1951), the discussion of "autonomy", "heteronomy" and "theonomy".

10. The essay appeared in 1966, published in Göttingen,
Vandenhoeck and Ruprecht.

11. See Ferré, Frederick, "Mapping the Logic of Models in
Science and Theology" in *The Christian Scholar*, vol. 46, 1963,
p. 9.

12. McGiffert, A. C., *Protestant Thought Before Kant*,
(New York, Harper and Row, 1961), p. 83. This work was originally published in 1911.

13. *Encyclopaedia of the Social Sciences*, 1930-1935, X, p.
564, article by Horace M. Kallen.

III: CORRESPONDENCE

1. The Karl Barth-Eduard Thurneysen Letters*

James D. Smart

In 1964, James Smart published an English
translation of those letters between these
friends which had already been published in
German. Drawn from the *Festschriften* in honor
of their seventieth birthdays in 1956 and in
1958, he entitled his volume *Revolutionary
Theology in the Making*.[1] Two years later an
edition of those same letters was published
in Germany, with an introduction by Eberhard
Busch.[2] The letters were called "Karl Barth's
reveille".[3]

More than those volumes, the edition of the
entire correspondence between Barth and
Thurneysen up to 1930--a third volume is
promised, to contain the remainder of their
letters--provides the vantage-point from
which one can see the development of Barth's
thought "in the rough", as he tests it in that
crucially important and fruitful medium of
human understanding: dialogue. And in that
dialogue one comes to know Barth--both as theologian and person--in a most intimate way.

It is for reasons of that intimate glimpse
that of the three reviews of volumes of
correspondence this one is placed first.

---

*Karl Barth-Eduard Thurneysen, *Briefwechsel 1913-1921*
(vol. I) and *Briefwechsel 1921-1930* (vol. II), Eduard Thurneysen, ed., (Zürich, TVZ, 1973 and 1974), pp. 543 and viii, 744.
These two are volumes 3 and 4 in the *Gesamtausgabe*.

In 1961 I tried to persuade Barth to visit the United States and Canada so that scholars and others on this side of the ocean might meet and hear him. I was certain that this would do much to overcome the false impressions and misconceptions that existed in many minds. At that time he insisted that he would "see North America only from heaven". As the next best thing I suggested a translation of the two sets of letters. He agreed at once. The book, about the only Barth biographical material available in English at that time, was published in 1964. Strangely it had a limited circulation. --Now, the definitive edition of this remarkable correspondence is before us.

Through the letters readers have the opportunity to visit with these two pioneering theologians during the years they were working their way out of the liberal Protestantism which had dominated the 19th century in Germany and which was singularly assured of its triumph at the time of the First World War. Even in the twenties--and in spite of the War--most bib- lical-scholars, church historians and theologians in general remained confident in their consensus of "assured results". One English scholar in his history of modern Christian thought saw all these lines of 19th century development coming to a climax in 1925! Even in 1913, before the War, these two pas- tors in their Swiss villages had begun to question the direc- tion in which Christian thinking, liberal and conservative alike, was going. Their questions dealt with more than theolo- gy. They looked at the whole order of life in the church, and beyond to the order of social and economic life in the human community. A few years ago it was often said that the 1914- 1918 War set Karl Barth thinking in a new direction. These letters take us back behind the War to May 1913 and show us the ferment already begun. They enable us to visit intimately with these two Christian thinkers during the 17 years in which they

were making their way step by step into a new era in theology,
church and world.

Although Karl Barth is widely known and Eduard Thurneysen
is almost unknown in the English-speaking world, their relationship was such that whatever one achieved, it was regarded
as a joint achievement. One wonders if there have ever been-
theologians whose thinking and writing have been so intimately
intermeshed as it was with them. They had been students together in Marburg. In 1911 Barth settled in Safenwil and in
1913 Thurneysen on the other side of the mountain, in Leutwil,
about ten miles away. Two and a half hours by foot took them
to each other's door. Often they met half-way at an inn to
discuss their sermons, their readings, their problems. When
they could not meet they wrote letters and sent each other
their sermons and other writings. They planned their studies
together and exchanged their findings. When they published
the first books of their sermons they did not differentiate
between authors because they regarded all the sermons as a
joint product.[4] Most remarkable is the fact that when Barth
was writing his commentary on Romans, he sent it piece by piece
to Thurneysen for criticism and revision. Often he incorporated whole paragraphs reformulated by his friend. Barth followed this procedure again in the 1921 edition of that work.
They laughed about the problem they were creating for future
investigators who would try to distinguish what was from the
pen of one and what from the pen of the other.

It is unfair that Thurneysen has been allowed to remain so
much in the shadow of Barth. There can be no question that
Barth is the more powerful and more profound theologian, with
a greater breadth of scholarship and a sharper eye for theological distinctions. That comes out clearly in the letters. But
in them we also see the two at the beginning. It was during
these years that Barth gradually achieved his breadth of schol-

ship and his discernment. A comparison of the first book of
essays and addresses by each shows how parallel they were until
1921 when Barth used his academic situation in Göttingen to
spread his theological wings.[5]

My own experience with the two in the early 1930's may be
interesting in this connection. I was attracted to them by
their second book of sermons *Come Holy Spirit*.[6] As a young
pastor who had found John Oman and John Baillie to be making
assumptions with which I could not agree, I was really grasped
by these sermons. Full of hope, I sent for Barth's *Römerbrief*,
but when it came I was so frustrated by it that I put it on the
shelf and left it there for many years. I had also secured
Thurneysen's addresses and they reached me in a way that
Barth's commentary did not. They became my doorway into this
theological development. Thinking they might do the same for
others, I spent a winter in my village pastorate translating
them. Because of Thurneysen's obscurity, they were not published. At my request Barth wrote an introduction to the
book. He said there that it was Thurneysen who had set him
moving theologically on the new road which he had been exploring ever since. It was Thurneysen who had brought him under
the influence of Blumhardt whose vivid eschatological perspective, waiting upon God, and whose faith in the risen Lord as
conqueror, issuing in strong social responsibility, had brought
a decisive change in his outlook.[7] Hermann Kutter, a disciple
of Blumhardt and a close friend of Thurneysen, helped continue
this influence. It was Thurneysen who introduced him to the
novels of Dostoevsky with their incisive critique of both
Western civilization and of the church in Western civilization.
It was in discussions with Thurneysen that he had begun to
grasp the dimensions of the theological revolution upon which
they embarked together.

The additional letters for the period 1913-1921, which

appear here, show much better than the ones published earlier how deeply both men were involved in the socialist and religious socialist movements of which Kutter and Ragaz provided differing forms of leadership. Barth, as usual, plunged in more deeply than Thurneysen, lecturing on socialism and its history to the social democratic party, becoming a party member, and helping to organize the workers in local factories. Thurneysen's pastorate, being more rural, presented a less embattled situation.

The result of the battle in Safenwil was an empty church and an enraged employer who did everything he could to make life difficult for Barth. Barth envied Thurneysen his ability to get on with people even while differing with them, what he called his "Johannine disposition", and his greater simplicity of expression which made his preaching and teaching more readily comprehensible to his people, both young and old.

There was conflict also with Ragaz and Kutter within the socialist movement. Ragaz made much too facile an identification of socialism with the advance of the kingdom of God on earth, while Barth and Thurneysen, equally committed to the transformation of the social and economic order as a demand which their loyalty to the kingdom made upon them, were unwilling to put the label "Christian" on any existing order. Kutter, with his better grasp of the distance between God and humankind, was closer to them, but when he became impatient with their involvement in the theological issues and controversies as "distractions from the real thing", they drew away from him.

It should not be forgotten that in 1913 both of these men were the products of the most liberal and scientific school of theology in Germany and Switzerland. They had been trained in the historical-critical interpretation of Scripture by Johannes Weiss and Adolf Jülicher in Marburg. Adolf von Harnack and

Wilhelm Herrmann, the leading Ritschlian theologians, had been
their teachers. Thurneysen's wedding gift to Barth in March
1913 was Ernst Troeltsch's *The Social Teaching of the Christian Churches*. Barth had spent an extra year in Marburg,
after completing his studies there, to assist Martin Rade in
editing the leading liberal journal *Christliche Welt*. By 1913
Barth had published in scholarly journals several large theological essays in the full stream of Ritschlian thought, though
they showed signs of questioning. It was several years before
they came to the realization they no longer belonged to the
school of Schleiermacher. Even in 1918 Barth could still parallel Plato with Old Testament prophets as anticipations of
the revelation to come in Jesus Christ. It is fascinating to
follow in the letters the transitions in their thought and to
note the influences which forced them ever forward.

It is this unresting movement that is most impressive in
the volumes. In one of his early addresses Barth says that
what makes the task of the theologian so difficult is that
he/she is trying to describe a bird in flight. The bird in
flight is the movement not of the theologian, but of God in
time. God is unresting in his activity in the world. Therefore, his truth cannot be captured in human formulations. A
static theology is a museum piece, but never can there be anything arbitrary in the theological movement. There is always
respect as well as repudiation in leaving the past behind.
When Brunner attacked Schleiermacher in his *Die Mystik und das
Wort*, Barth reminded him that one must first understand what,
in the providence of God, Schleiermacher *was*; on one occasion
Barth suggested that he might have said what Schleiermacher
said had he lived in Schleiermacher's time. All human existence, including all theological standpoints, are relativized
by the radical perspective of eschatology so that, at the same
time, theologians, in spite of their intense seriousness about

the issues, are kept from taking themselves too seriously. In conversation with a Jesuit theologian, Erich Przywara, Barth wondered whether, in his situation and with his past, he would not have come out where Przywara did. It is this element in Barth which enables him, in his history of the nineteenth century Protestant theology, to interpret sympathetically theologians with whom he is in basic disagreement.

Anyone accustomed to lumping together the members of the so-called "Barthian school" of the 20s and thinking Barth rude in breaking with Brunner and Gogarten in 1934, will be surprised to learn what serious differences had appeared before 1925. They were solidly united in what they opposed and in their determination that there should be a new and different future for theology and church, but they were not united in shaping that future. Barth saw a peril in the attempts of Gogarten, Brunner and Bultmann to provide a philosophical preparation in differing ways for the reception and interpretation of the gospel. He was not hostile to philosophy per se; he recognized that theology, his own included, had in it philophical presuppositions. He made no secret of his fondness for Platonism. But a philosophical prolegomena to the construction of a Christian theology could so easily mean the betrayal of the gospel to the world order for which the philosophy was a validation. He scented new forms of natural revelation in Gogarten's and Brunner's "order of creation" which became, in Brunner's thought, the basis of validating what could only be called an outdated concept of Christendom and, in the case of Gogarten, permitted him to support for a time the German Christian Movement who actively backed the Nazis.

Two decisive moments in Barth's development stand out clearly in these letters. The first, in a letter of September 4, 1914 (p. 9f, vol. I), might not be noticed were it not for later comments on it by Barth. Letters from German friends, such as Martin Rade, had shown the prevalence of an uncritical war-spirit. Barth comments: "The absolute ideas of the gospel are simply suspended for the time being and in the meantime a Germanic war-theology is put to work with Christian trimmings, consisting of a lot of talk about sacrifice and the like. Sufficient proof that those ideas were nothing more than a varnish and not a firm inward possession of that "Christian World" Christianity.[8] It is all so sad! Marburg and German civilization have lost something in my eyes, and that for good, by this collapse" (p. 10). A question mark was set against the whole theological tradition in which until now he had had his life. From this point on, until the very end of his life, his endeavour was to construct a theology which would not be betrayed by its cultural and national environment.

The second turning point which has not had adequate notice came in January 1920. Barth and Thurneysen began reading the works of Franz Overbeck,[9] professor of Church History at Basel late in the 19th century and a close friend of Nietzsche. Much has been made of the influence of Søren Kierkegaard in 1919 in setting Barth thinking in such a new direction that he had to rewrite the whole of his commentary on Romans. Kierkegaard certainly made his contribution, but in these letters it is Overbeck, back to back with Blumhardt, who is the decisive influence through his radical critique of the whole of modern developments in the ecclesial and cultural expression of Christianity.

These letters make us once more conscious of the fact that this major theological movement of our century which changed the character of biblical scholarship and brought a systematic theology back to the centre of the theological curriculum originated not in any university but in two village churches. And the originators were without the highly prized Doctor of Philosophy or Doctor of Theology. They were two village pastors who took seriously their responsibility as preachers and teachers to be critical theologians. Struggling with the task of making the decisive content of Scripture meaningful to the people, they inaugurated a new era in the history of the Christian church. If anyone doubts that it is a new era, let him/her try today to read any of the typical products of the theology of the twenties.

NOTES

1. The book was published by John Knox Press, Richmond.

2. Karl Barth-Eduard Thurneysen, *Ein Briefwechsel aus der Frühzeit der dialektischen Theologie,* (München and Hamburg, Siebenstern Taschenbuch Verlag, 1966).

3. Eberhard Busch's introductory essay to the German edition (see Note 2 above) was translated into English and appears under the title "Karl Barth's Reveille" in *Canadian Journal of Theology,* vol. 16, 1970, pp. 165-174.

4. The two volumes referred to are *Suchet Gott, so werdet ihr leben,* published in 1917 by Bäschlin Verlag, Berne, republished in 1928 by Chr. Kaiser Verlag, Munich, and *Komm Schöpfer Geist!* published in 1924 by Kaiser, Munich.

5. The first book of essays Barth published was *Das Wort Gottes und die Theologie,* translated into English as *The Word of God and the Word of Man,* (Munich, Chr. Kaiser Verlag, 1924, ET. 1928). Thurneysen's first volume of essays was entitled *Das Wort Gottes und die Kirche,* (Munich, Chr. Kaiser Verlag, 1927). It never appeared in English. Note the suggestive difference in the German titles: Barth speaking of *Theologie* and Thurneysen of *Kirche*--church, as the focus of attention relating to God's Word.

6. Cf. note 4 on original publication data. This volume was published in an English translation by Round Table Press, New York, in 1933. One notes--with satisfaction--that a new English edition appeared again in 1979: Grand Rapids, Michigan, Wm. B. Eerdmans Publishing Company.

7. Just recently a remarkable compendium of the Blumhardt's thought has appeared in English and deserves to be mentioned here. *Thy Kingdom Come--A Blumhardt Reader,* Vernard Eller, ed., (Grand Rapids, Michigan, Wm. B. Eerdmans Publishing Co., 1980), pp. xx, 179.

8. Barth alludes to the influential paper *Christliche Welt,* (Christian World) on the editorial staff of which he had once worked.

9. The reference is to pp. 364-365 of vol. I of these letters.

2: The Barth-Bultmann Correspondence*

H.-Martin Rumscheidt

Eduard Thurneysen and Rudolf Bultmann are the
only "members" of the movement outsiders dubbed
"dialectical theology" with whom Barth had sustained an extensive correspondence. In this
volume, as in the ones discussed in the previous
chapter, the exchanges grant insight into the
growth of Barth's thought, into the manner of
its delineation from, but also its indebtedness
to the thought of others. There is more delineation here than indebtedness; yet there
is also testimony of a friendship which, in
spite of many unsuccessful attempts to secure
a real understanding one of another, remained
firm.

The volume also accompanies a period of "secular"
history which posed incisive problems. Thus,
the letters clarify as well the stance of theological existence in a time of wild idolatry,
contributing also to our understanding of not
only Barth and Bultmann, but also of the issues
of the Church-Struggle.

---

*Karl Barth-Rudolf Bultmann, *Briefwechsel, 1922-1966*,
Bernd Jaspert, ed. (Zürich, TVZ, 1971), pp. xii, 376. This is
volume 1 of the *Gesamtausgabe*.
This review is based on an address delivered at the Annual
Meeting of the American Academy of Religion in 1976 at St.
Louis and at the Third Karl Barth Colloquium at Toronto in 1977.
--Portions of this review were first published in *Religious
Studies Review*--3/3 (1977), 151-154, and are reprinted here
with permission of the publishers, Council on the Study of Re-
ligion.

The correspondence between these theological leaders
spans a period, the beginning and end of which (1922 and 1966)
can be signalled in terms of two slogans: "God after God" and
"Death of God". Barth's second edition of his *Römerbrief*,
which appeared seven months before the first item of the two
men's correspondence, ushered in the "God after God" theology;[1]
the last item of their correspondence coincides with the ze-
nith of the "Death of God" theology. From "God after God" to
the "Death of God" and in between demythologization, the Third
Reich and the continued collapse of Western Civilization: a
book not only of friendship and of theological probings by
two men, but also of the history they shared.

Of the 98 letters and cards in this volume, 20 letters
and 33 cards are by Bultmann, 25 letters and 10 cards by
Barth. Eleven items by Barth were lost in 1969 on the way
from Marburg to the editor. Dr. Jaspert has provided excellent biographical and literary notes and added a most valuable
supplement of 40 letters, cards, public declarations, memo-
randa and autobiographical sketches. A 50-page register facil-
atates the use of the book for research purposes.

As a reviewer in *Times Literary Supplement* put it, these
letters do not offer much which people well acquainted with
Barth and Bultmann do not already know. That Barth painted
the verbal picture of J. A. T. Robinson as a man who spooned
the foam of three glasses of beer, one labelled R. B. (ultmann),
another P. T. (illich) and the third D. B. (onhoeffer), then
mixed the foam together and presented the concoction as the
finally discovered theological miracle-drink (p. 205 f.), was
known at least two years before the publication of this volume.
But there is a host of significant (and not so significant)
items of information, fact and interpretation which, because
they are now all under one cover, make the book valuable.
There are, for example, two autobiographical sketches by Barth

and Bultmann. Barth's, composed in 1927 and expanded in 1935
and 1946, makes a fine prolegomenon to the three *Christian Century* "How I Changed My Mind" articles.[2] Bultmann's was first
published by Schubert Ogden in his 1960 edition of Bultmann's
Existence and Faith, expanded for Charles Kegley's *The Theology of Rudolf Bultmann* (1966) and expanded again in a sketch
about Bultmann's relation to Marburg (included in this volume).
On the human, so very human sorrow expressed by Bultmann to
Barth that after all, they could not spend their family holidays in the same resort in Northern Germany because "my wife
threatened at the last moment to strike: I must not spend the
holidays with you, since this would take me away from the family, I would be theologizing all the time and get no rest at
all". Bultmann continues "Whether it would have been that bad,
I do not know, but I gave in" (p. 46).

There is a fascinating letter by Bonheoffer's cousin, H.
C. von Hase, in which he reflects on his cousin's relationship
to and fascination with Barth and Bultmann (P. 91f). Then
there is that delightful touch of Barth's humour, reacting of
all things to the solemn dignity of a Scottish honorary doctorate. Bultmann was to receive an honorary D.D. from St. Andrew's
University. Believing Barth had already been so honored by
that university (it had, in fact, been Glasgow University; two
years after Bultmann Barth received the St. Andrew's D.D.) he
asked about proper etiquette. Do I make a speech? Do I wear
tails? Must I purchase the doctor's regalia? Barth replied,
No speech is necessary, but someone will present a *laudatio*
and then you must smile every time your name is mentioned. The
university will lend you a gown. Afterwards a hood will be offered to you for purchase. Foolishly, I bought mine for four
pounds! But I have sported it here for all university functions and the media people believe me when I say that I am a
papal legate. During the ceremony you will kneel and someone

will mumble something incomprehensible in Latin over your head.
But the whole event will be real fun--which we all need so
dearly these days (p. 160f). That was written in March 1935.
Finally, what would those adept in interpreting symbolism make
of the curious sequence of streetnames where the two men
lived? Bultmann moved from Hainweg (Grave Road) to Friedrich
Str. (Frederick Street) to Bismarck Str. to Calvinweg; Barth
from Nikolausbergerweg (St. Nicholas Mountain Road) to Himmel-
reichallee (Kingdom of Heaven Avenue) to Siebengebirgstrasse
(Seven Mountains Road--a reference to a mountain range in Germany) to Pilgrimstr.; to St. Alban Ring (St Alban Circle) and,
finally, to Bruderholz (the Woods of Brothers).

Friends and strangers, or: attempts to understand the
other--this is a formula-like description of what pervades the
whole correspondence. Whether 'friends' describes more accurately how things stood between them at one time and 'strangers'
at another, the wish to understand the other, precisely because
he was genuinely respected and honored, manifests itself
throughout the book. And because both Barthians and Bultman-
nians (or should one even say now Barthniks and Bultmaniacs?)
react to one another's critiques of their masters with disdain
or scorn, it is good to see the very real humanity, the insistence of both to stay in contact, the congeniality of that contact (although it always remained at the *Sie*, never at the *Du*
level) and the need both felt to meet personally so as to have
that talk to identify and possibly heal the *theological* breach
between them. No *rabies theologorum* here; would that the
epigones did likewise!

The first documented contact in writing between the two
(who met at Marburg in 1908/1909) was in March, 1911, when
Peter Barth (Karl's younger brother) sent a card from the famous annual conference at Aarau. "From our beer hall table
we, your Swiss friends, send warm greetings--Peter Barth, F.

Zimmerlin, Alphons Koechlin, A. Kind, Karl Barth, Eduard
Thurneysen, Fr. Hock, G. Wieser" (p. vi f). Bultmann and Barth
met again in 1919 at the Tambach Conference (where Barth gave
his now famous address "The Christian's Place in Society"[3]).
From then on the contact was steady; of the 98 published letters and cards, 91 predate World War II. The war permitted no
contacts at all and the correspondence resumes in 1950.[4]
Of note is a seven year gap. In 1952 Barth published his famous Bultmann interpretation attempt, to which the latter wrote
a very lengthy reply and to which Barth responded. There was
no correspondence until 1959. There is no doubt theological
differences led to this reduction in contacts.

An unceasing determination to understand the other was
the precondition for the open, sometimes sharp, but always
fair dialogue in their correspondence. For those who did not
study under them the book is easily a better key to these men's
theologies than much of the current secondary literature.

What produced this rare kind of relationship in which,
despite critical material differences, the two firmly believed
themselves to be friends to the last and in which, despite
their very clear good will toward each other, they were theological strangers even from the first? Why does Barth, asses-
sing the way things were between them, come to the following
conclusion: "Is it clear to you where you and I are? It looks
to me like a whale and an elephant who met in utter bewilderment on some oceanic shore. In vain that the one sends a
stream of water high up into the air. In vain that the other
beckons, now amicably, then menacingly, with his trunk. They
lack a common key to what both, each one from his proper element and each in his own language, obviously and so anxiously
want to say to the other" (p. 196; the letter is dated Dec. 24,
1952).

It is worthwhile to follow the whale and the elephant from

the outset of the correspondence. Bultmann had written a
lengthy review of the second edition of the *Römerbrief* and
sent it to Barth before it was printed.[5] He said that the review contained several reservations which he would much rather
discuss personally with Barth in order "if possible to reach
an understanding" (p. 3). The areas of which Bultmann was
critical were historical-philological exegesis and precision
of terminology. Barth responded to the review, but alas! the
response was one of the letters lost in 1969. Bultmann ac-
cepted some of the corrections Barth wished him to make and incorporated them in the published review. A few months later,
the *Römerbrief* appeared in a third edition, the preface to
which was almost in its entirety a reply to Bultmann's review.[6]
Barth called it a "friendly reception" but took issue with two
aspects concerning exegesis. The exegete must not remain
satisfied with a "commentary *on*", but press on to "speak *with*"
the apostle. After having heard all the "other spirits" which
raise their voices in the biblical writings, he must see how
all that has been heard stands in relation to the true subject
matter, the Spirit of Christ, the *krisis* of all spirits. Bultmann, to whom Barth had sent a gift copy of that edition, an-
swered in a long letter (pp. 8-13). He indicated there was
really no essential difference between their points of view regarding exegesis, although exegetical praxis would show variant
results. "There is a far more basic difference," he continued.
"It has become increasingly more obvious to me that your relation to the science of history is not as strong as your relation to idealistic philosophy. Just as Plato's philosophy
leads to the boundaries of the human, so does history for
Wilhelm von Humboldt. Where historical criticism is exercised,
not for the sake of determining causal relations, but in the
service of self-reflection, as a method of never ending questioning, it leads from hypothesis to hypothesis and finally to

the question of the ultimate hypothesis. For me Hellenistic
mysticism or Jewish legalism, etc., are not facts of historical interest by which one can 'explain' a certain Pauline
statement. . .but manifestations of specific spiritual positions, the discovery of whose exertions in the sources draws
the exegete into dialogue with them and lets them ask of him
the decisive questions" (p. 9 f.). It is clear in retrospect
that Barth and Bultmann were forced to part theological company on the aim of historical criticism. In 1922 Barth
could not clearly see why such a view caused him unease. As
it was, this discussion about the *Römerbrief* lead *für eine
Weile zu einer beträchtlichen theologischen Nähe* (to a temporary but significant theological closeness) between him and
Bultmann, as Barth put it in 1963.[7] This proximity is evident
in Barth's letter of October 9, 1923 where he writes: "If you
could get me called to Marburg, please do under no circumstances neglect to do so" (p. 18). And in his letter to
Thurneysen, March 4, 1924, after a conference at Marburg, he
says: "Marburg has really become once again one of those
places on the map of Central Europe on which one's eyes may
rest with satisfaction".[8] His applause of Bultmann's essay
Die liberale Theologie und die jüngste theologische Bewegung
of 1924[9] is an indication of Barth's satisfaction. He called
it "a *Götterdämmerung*" (p. 27). Bultmann's own positive relation to Barth can be deduced from the fact the Heidegger expressed through him the desire to welcome Barth in Marburg
(p. 33).

Yet underneath it there were questions. Bultmann was to
give a lecture at Göttingen and Barth urged they should main-
tain a common front in public. He wanted to know beforehand
what Bultmann had to say so that he would not be tripped into
saying something against Bultmann in the heat of the discussion
following the lecture (p. 38). What Bultmann wanted to say was

that a theological exegesis of Scripture was an impossible
possibility (p. 35). This would, of course, reveal to the
alert the differences between the two men. Barth asked only
that Bultmann not attend his classes the day after the guest-
lecture, because he was giving a theological exegesis of Colos-
sians (p. 39). After that visit on February 6, 1925, Barth
wrote Thurneysen "Bultmann told me my terminology is not precise (and that is not really disputable). I told him his
thinking is too anthropological-Kierkegaardian-Lutheran (plus
Gogartian), "To speak of God is to speak of the human", that
his relation to the Scriptures is outrageously eclectic and
that he was not quite rid of his historicist egg-shells. . .I
see him in great proximity to Gogarten but, as with that man,
say to myself: ten times that rather than Holl".[10] Upon his
completion of *Jesus*,[11] Bultmann wrote Barth that he feared
what the latter might think of it (p. 44); Barth expressed his
premonitions about the work to Thurneysen: "after what he
told me, I do not expect much good from it".[12] Whatever the
expectations and reactions were,[13] the two travelled together
to a major conference at Danzig, where Barth spoke on Philip-
pians 3 and Bultmann on New Testament eschatology. At a stop-
over in Berlin, the two had a good meal "in a well known
gourmet restaurant. Barth drank cool beer and I, slightly
warmed red wine. He said he would cure me of that " (p. 60).
On that trip Bultmann had the galleys of his review of Barth's
Die Auferstehung der Toten[14] with him and the two discussed
the critique (p. 62). By the end of 1926 there are signs of
anxiety over the sensed, but not firmly conceptualized, differences. Bultmann wrote: "It is really important to me that
we finally come to a definite understanding of the opposition
between us which manifests itself in all kinds of differences"
(p. 63). In April, 1927 he wrote: "I am quite depressed by
the lack of exchange between us. Münster lies so much off the

beaten track. Could you not stop off at Marburg on one of your trips? Would you like me to arrange for a lecture here? As you surround yourself in silence, I almost fear that you have given up on me. Even though I believe that in the closer theological relationship between Gogarten and me, in opposition to you, the old cleavage between Lutherans and Calvinists is at work, I do hope that feud need not be renewed because of it. Our oneness appears to me to be much greater and more decisive. I also hope that you do not think me unteachable and, therefore, it would grieve me if you let our exchange just drop off. So, do write again" (p. 68).

Barth responded openly and in real friendship: "Do not interpret my stubborn silence as wickedness. You don't do that, I know, and I am really grateful to you. You see, with me it is simply that at this time (and it might last a little longer) I do not see through everything which seems to be in the air between you, Gogarten and me. . . .Somehow it must be the old, never really settled Lutheran-Reformed controversies, which make problems for us from both sides. Perhaps they will lead to a real explosion in *Zwischen den Zeiten*. But right now, apart from all tactical reasons which may also be meaningful, I have the need to carry on my work in as thetical a way as possible and at the same time leave you and Gogarten time to develop more clearly what it is you really want to say. . . . For now I do not wish to raise foolish questions and objections. . .and run along my course just as you all do, too" (p. 70). He continued by expressing his urgent wish to meet Bultmann face to face again, assuring him that he has no desire to give up on him and concludes: "I am so glad and grateful when I am not given up" (*ibid*).

After the appearance of Barth's *Die christliche Dogmatik im Entwurf* Bultmann sent Barth a long list of questions and criticisms of that work. They were not meant for publication

and were never published. These *gravamina*, as Barth called
them (p. 78) were, for Bultmann, expressions of critical gratitude (p. 80). The book is "a beginning in genuine work in
dogmatics" (*ibid*). Bultmann suggested one shortcoming--the
critical discussion of the work of Barth's friends, especially
of Gogarten--which must be corrected in what he assumes will
of course happen: the second edition of the book. "What is
more important is that you have rejected the (latent, but radical) discussion of theology with modern philosophy and have
taken over naively the old ontology of patristic and scholastic
dogmatics. . . You sovereignly ignore modern philosophical
work, and hence, above all, phenomenology. . .It seems to me
that you are guided by the worry that theology might allow
itself to be made dependent on philosophy. You try to avoid
that by ignoring philosophy and the price you pay for that is
that you fall victim to a past philosophy. Since faith is the
faith of a believer, that is to say of an existing human being
(I can also phrase it: since the justified is the *sinner*),
dogmatics can speak only in the concepts of existential ontology which, deriving from a preceding understanding of existence
(*Daseinsverständnis*), are elaborated by philosophy" (p. 80 f.).
"That I have learned, am learning and continue, hopefully to
learn decisive matters from you, I do not need to emphasize.
I am the one who receives from you, the pupil, albeit the critical pupil. More important to me than critique is the gratitude I owe you. My critique itself is guided by the conviction
that I am *at one* with you in the matter which you defend in
your dogmatics" (p. 82).

Barth's response to that letter was very appreciative.
"It was a festive moment yesterday, when I unrolled your scroll
with its notes. I was quite aware that for the first time I
was about to read something against my dogmatics which I shall
not be able to avoid considering very seriously. Please accept

very hearty thanks for all your great troubles which shall not
have been taken in vain" (p. 83).

Yet Barth senses immediately that what Bultmann suggests
in terms of criticism demands no less than a very radical
"transformation of the spiritual *habitus* with which I approach
my work. . .It is as if you wished to give a more pleasing
appearance to a wild and misshapen tree (that is how I saw
myself in the light of your critique) by placing a straight
pole next to it" (*ibid*).

Barth just has no genuine interest any more to discuss
theology with Gogarten. (This in a letter of June 12, 1928,
and not only after the advent of the Third Reich.) "What you
ask of me regarding philosophy just is not my thing. I shall
not explain in principle what you call my ignoring philosophy.
It is possible that someone else can do better regarding the
precision of conceptuality. You see, no philosophy has moved
in on me as Heidegger's obviously has on you so that I should
be under the compulsion to measure and to purify my thinking
in light of your standards. Furthermore, I now have an abhorrence of the game of theology to do things right above all
to the philosophy of its time and in the process forget its
own subject-matter. . .My course in the *Römerbrief* and now in
the *Dogmatik* is this: when it came to the subject with which,
as I see it, the Bible and the history of dogma concern themselves I made use right and left of 'concepts' which seemed
most suitable to me. I gave no thought to the problem of a
preestablished harmony between the subject-matter and those defined concepts, simply because I had my hands full doing something else. . .my anxious question is whether I will be suc-
cessfully domesticated or whether it is worthwhile for me to
purchase an unambiguous conceptuality from the phenomenologists
for the rest of my life. . .I admit this looks like dreadful
dilettantism. . .but it is my concern to hear the voice of the

Church and the Bible under all circumstances and to let it be
heard, even if, lacking something better, I have to be Aristo-
telian for a while. . .I do concede that it would be good for
me to understand the art which I watch you practise with admiration. . .but it could be that your critique (*Appell*) has
its value in pointing out those limits beyond which I cannot
proceed" (p. 84 f).

Bultmann was pleased with Barth's positive response but
could not help wishing that Barth had as great a desire as he
for a critical dialogue and understanding (p. 88).

In early 1930 it is becoming apparent that their differences are fundamental and well nigh insurmountable. On January
20 of that year Barth had given a guest lecture at Marburg and
had several good personal talks with Bultmann. "It was so good
to be back in your house and I am grateful for it" he writes
(p. 100). But he admits, he left quite grieved about Marburg.
"From my point of view the meaning. . .of your endeavors looks
like a grandiose return to the flesh-pots of Egypt. What I
mean is that you are all busy with understanding faith once
again as a human possibility or, if you like, as founded on a
human possibility and thereby deliver theology anew into the
hands of philosophy. Of course, you do so in a new and quite
different manner from the theology of the 19. century. . .
Whenever one plays with the possibility of a natural theology,
and is assiduous in theologizing within the framework of a non-
theologically gained pre-understanding, one inevitably ends up
in such contortions and reactionary corners no better than
the liberalisms of the others. . . How I wished to be able
personally to see things differently and to know myself more
at one with you" (p. 101 f).

At that time Barth was deeply involved in his study of 19.
century Protestant theology and it looked to him that what had
become called 'dialectical theology' was in danger of bringing

back exactly those things that it had believed itself to be
opposing. "It would be so good," his letter continues, "if
you were able to comfort and assure me that it is not nearly
so dangerous and that you and I are together as before, but I
am afraid you cannot tell me so. It could just be that what I
understand by 'the Word of God' was never a concern for you in
this way. . ." (p. 102).

Bultmann was not able to reply at length at the time but
urged Barth to agree to a meeting, at Brunner's and Gogarten's
suggestion, where the four, plus Thurneysen, could talk things
over and really see where they all stood. Barth replied that
he would gladly come. Regrettably the meeting never occurred.
A year later it seemed to Barth that such a meeting, now that
he was much clearer about all their essential positions,
would have uncovered the painful realization how very far apart
they all were and that, basically, there had never been a real
oneness. Between Barth and Gogarten and Barth and Brunner
something decisive had gone awry. It would be very difficult
to meet and discuss (p. 118).

Bultmann was puzzled by that assessment. He asked Barth
why he was so suspicious. "Don't you think I seriously want
to find out what you have against my work? Where our opposition arises and where I have possibly gone wrong? How you
substantiate the charges in your letter?" (p. 123). He went
on to urge Barth to express publicly where he thought Bultmann
betrayed theology. This did not occur until 21 years later.[15]
Barth, replying to that letter of Bultmann's, suggested that
both should continue in their own work, have some good personal
discussions in the meantime and in this manner learn to understand better what the other really wanted (p. 129). Bultmann,
however, took this to be an indication of Barth's faint interest in exploring Bultmann's work (p. 135). He believed there
was no genuinely basic difference between them, as Barth thought.

Then came 1933 and all that. Their letters now rarely
touch on theological issues between them, but are concerned
with matters arising from the state's problems with Barth and
the Confessing Church. At one point Bultmann insists on how
irreplaceable Barth is (p. 148). At another he admits to
Barth how hurt he was when the latter said he had expected
Bultmann to join the *German Christians*. Still, he added, it
was a sign of how much Barth misunderstood him (p. 151). Barth
conceded that, but asked him, after apologizing for that expec-
tation, to explain how, in Bultmann's theology, that step
would not have been consistent (p. 153).

Before Barth was forced out of Germany there was one more
occasion via the *Deutsche Reichspost* when the growing separation showed up. Bultmann sent Barth two sermons, asking that
they be considered for inclusion in the series *Theologische
Existenz heute*, which Barth edited. In an accompanying letter
he stated his impressions about Barth's own sermons. "You in-
terrogate the text according to a dogmatic formula so that it
cannot speak with its own voice. After a few sentences one
knows everything else you are going to say and one asks occasionally how you get that out of the next verses. . .You will
sense heresy in my faith and understanding, but I think Paul
addressed himself differently to the existence of his hearers
than you. . .namely in such a way that their existence became
transparent to them under the impact of his words" (p. 163).

Barth did send the sermons back with the comment that
Christ was not made known in them whereas the believing person
was explicated. I find them boring, Barth wrote, and not beyond what one hears from "positive Ritschlians" (p. 164).
Then he identifies what it is that lies between them: the difference in the relation between christology and anthropology
(p. 165).

After the War their correspondence is made up of five

short and two very lengthy items. The latter occupy 33 of 40
pages. These two deal with Barth's famous (infamous?) study
Rudolf Bultmann--Ein Versuch, ihn zu verstehen.[16] Bultmann
took five days to write his reply to the pamphlet (November 11
to 15, 1952). Barth responded on December 24 that year. It
is utterly essential for the discussion of the relationship
between the theologies of these two men that those two letters
are read with Barth's *Versuch* and his other public discussions
about Bultmann's work.[17] For one, it will not only illuminate
many existing attempts to understand Barth's *Attempt* as short
circuits, but will also prevent whatever Barthians and Bult-
mannians still exist from prematurely adopting inflexible
stances toward one another and the 'masters'. In addition,
the letters place the *Attempt* into the context of three decades
of fermentation and thereby illuminate both the man writing it,
the man and the thought to whom it was addressed and the actual
remarks made about them. It is, I believe, high time to re-
assess the pamphlet.

One simply has to make reference to the personal touches
which are sprinkled throughout this correspondence of November
and December 1952. Barth had sent the work to Bultmann,
autographed it and added a quotation from the finale of Mozart's
The Marriage of Figaro: "angel, forgive me." Bultmann began
his letter "I was tempted to reply with a quotation from
Mozart's *Don Giovanni*: 'Commendatore (K. B.)--Repent, wicked
man! Don Giovanni (R. B.)--No, you old crank!' But I resisted,
lest I should tempt you to reply in the Commendatore's words
'Your time is up'" (p. 169). And he ends the letter, five days
later: "But now let me conclude by continuing your *Figaro*
quotation: 'How could I be angry? My heart, it speaks for
you' and by adding the last line of *Figaro*: 'Let all anger be
forever banished'" (p. 192).

Barth wrote Bultmann twice more. Bultmann sent Barth a

card for his eightieth birthday. "From old Marburg also shall come a greeting for your birthday. Good health and confident courage for the new year wishes you with all his heart your old Rudolf Bultmann" (p. 207).

The attempts to understand each other remained unresolved. What their public utterances would not readily show becomes blatantly apparent in the *Correspondence*. Neither was ever really sure he knew precisely what the other meant. Why, then, did neither make a determined effort to get to the root of these theological differences? How could friends, and both believed genuinely that that is what they were, live out their relationship with a cloud hanging over them? A psychological or a biographical investigation of this aspect would be fascinating. The theological answer to that matter most likely is that the friends were strangers to each other in the one issue to which their minds and major efforts were devoted: the proclamation of the Christ.

NOTES

1. The slogan is borrowed from the excellent book *God after God* by Robert Jenson, subtitled: *The God of the Past and the God of the Future,* seen in the Work of Karl Barth, (Indianapolis, The Bobbs-Merrill Company, 1969).

2. These articles are conveniently brought together in John Godsey, ed. Karl Barth, *How I Changed My Mind,* (Richmond, John Knox Press, 1966).

3. The address was published in *Das Wort Gottes und die Theologie,* (Munich, Chr. Kaiser Verlag, 1924), pp. 33 to 69. E.T. *The Word of God and the Word of Man,* (Boston, The Pilgrim Press, 1928), pp. 272-327.

4. They met each other in person on August 31, 1945 at Marburg and again on September 21, 1948.

5. The review is available in English in J. M. Robinson, ed., *The Beginnings of Dialectic Theology,* (Richmond, John Knox Press, 1968), pp. 100 to 120.

6. Karl Barth, *The Epistle to the Romans*, (London, Oxford University Press, 1933), pp. 15 to 20.

7. Karl Barth, *Der Römerbrief*, reprint of the first edition, (Zurich, TVZ, 1963), in the preface to the reprint-edition.

8. Karl Barth-Eduard Thurneysen, *Briefwechsel, 1921-1930,* (Zurich, TVZ, 1974), p. 231. - This is the second of the two volumes reviewed in the previous chapter.

9. Rudolf Bultmann, *Glauben und Verstehen,* vol. I, (Tübingen, J. C. B. Mohr [Paul Siebeck] 1933), pp. 1 to 25.

10. Karl Barth-Eduard Thurneysen, *Briefwechsel 1921-1930,* p. 306f.

11. Tübingen, J. C. B. Mohr [Paul Siebeck], 1926, E.T. *Jesus and the Word,* (New York, Scribner's Sons, 1958).

12. Karl Barth-Eduard Thurneysen, *Briefwechsel 1921-1930*, p. 307.

13. Bultmann explains in a long letter (pp. 63 ff.) what he had set out to do in the book *Jesus*.

14. (Munich, Chr. Kaiser Verlag, 1924), E.T. *The Resurrection of the Dead*, (London, Hodder and Stoughton, 1933).

15. See note 16.

16. Karl Barth, *Rudolf Bultmann--Ein Versuch ihn zu verstehen, Theologische Studien*, vol. 34, (Zurich, TVZ, 1952). E.T. *Rudolf Bultmann--An Attempt to Understand Him*, in Hans-Werner Bartsch, ed., *Kerygma and Myth*, vol. II, (London, S.P. C.K.), pp. 83 to 132.

17. Such as in *Church Dogmatics*, vols. III/2 and IV, *passim*.

3: Letters 1961 to 1968*

James J. Buckley

In 1961 Barth retired from his academic
position. Even though the flow of publications slowed considerably, his participation
and interest in theological, ecclesial, political and cultural questions continued un-
abated. The correspondence in this volume,
letters by Karl Barth and letters to him,
throws light on the strength of his participation, the thrust of it and its impact.
There is a good deal of personal-biographical
matter as well as concerns of others who de-
sired Barth's guidance for them.

It is very appropriate that the last volume
to be reviewed here should be given over to
an intimate glimpse at Barth in his final
years. For here that unique place of retro-
spection is given to us, from which one can
venture out, venture backward into Barth's
work and, thereby, forward into theology.

Those interested in novel uses of Barth for church and
world are currently faced with a complicated but exciting array of possibilities. This volume of letters does not tell
whether complications or excitement will prevail, but it does
pose the problem in a sharp form. Fangmeier and Stoevesandt

---

*Karl Barth, *Briefe 1961-1968*, Jürgen Fangmeier and Hinrich Stoevesandt, eds., (Zürich, TVZ, 1975), pp. xxviii, 600.
This is volume 6 in the *Gesamtausgabe*.

have done excellent work in selecting and annotating 329 letters from the last seven and one half years of Barth's life.
17 letters to Barth, relevant to the main collection, are ap-
pended as is a 26 page index of Scripture passages, names,
concepts and books referred to in the main letters. Both the
unity and diversity of this volume raise an important question
and make this collection a valuable contribution to the study
of Barth, his neighbours, and his times.

The main strands of unity are provided by a fact that
sets this volume apart from the others of the collected edition published to date.[1] It is the first tome devoted solely
to providing first-hand information about the last years of
Barth's life. The author himself provides the main strand of
continuity and here we find some interesting glimpses of the
interaction of an 'old man', as he did not hesitate to refer
to himself, with people and circumstances near and far.

The letters begin with the month of Barth's 75. birthday,
May 1961. They end with a note from December 6, 1968, four
days before his death. They cover years which were anything
but the 'rest' which Barth sometimes wished they had been.
His retirement came in 1961 but had to be put off because of
the "political difficulties" (p. 11) over the choice of his
successor. When he finally did retire, he proceeded to travel
to the United States (1962), to Copenhagen and Paris (1963),
to Rome (1966)[2] and elsewhere. Such journeys were interrupted
by various domestic matters, including a broken arm (1962),
prostate operations (1964 and 1965), a stroke (1964), pneumo-
nia (1968) and discomforting intestinal ailments. Indeed, his
journey to Rome seemed to be one of the few times his "bowels
and bladder" enjoyed, as he put it, good "ecumenical" relations
(p. 357).

Most of the activity of these years was considerably less
dramatic. Even Barth's literary output no longer took its pre-

vious massive form. God and the angels, he said, wanted to know if he could live a little of what he had written about for so many years (p. 317). His literary productivity was 'moderated' to include a fragment of the *Church Dogmatics*, a few articles, some addresses, sermons, conversations and letters, including those in this volume.

Letters, of course do not tell the whole story and these are no exception. The broader story of these years is better gleaned from Eberhard Busch's *Karl Barth, His Life from Letters and Autobiographical Texts*.[3] However, letters are an indispensable part of the story, as the subtitle of that book indicates. For example, Barth may have abandoned his autobiography in part because of its tiresome *Ichbezogenheit* (p. 389-reference to self), but he has little hesitancy to be candid about his own desires, moods, and thoughts in these letters. This occurs throughout the 'circular letters' which Barth sent in 1961, 1964, 1966, 1967, and 1968 to the many who sent him "eatable, drinkable, smokable, readable and audible gifts of all kinds" on his birthdays (p. 475).

But his various reactions are also scattered throughout other letters. Thus, he reflects, but never broods over, his own past in some interesting ways. He sometimes wishes it could have been quite different, perhaps the life of a universal literary genius like Ernst Wolf (p. 17), or the life of an historian (p. 70) or a politician (p. 487). His socialism at Safenwil is a vivid part of his memory, even though he insists that his involvement in socialism was primarily theological and practical and not 'ideological' (p. 487 and p. 152). The changes he underwent during and after his pastorate came, he says, "of themselves" and without the "Angst" he sees when today's youth struggle with admittedly similar problems (p. 449). Along other lines, he does not hesitate to mention the depressions which periodically engulfed him during the retirement years (pp. 36, 118, 324, 427, 515).

The most vivid outburst comes in a letter to Helmut Gollwitzer in 1962, after Heinrich Ott was chosen for Barth's
chair. "In the face of the pressures of our theological ex-
istentialists, the longer I go on the more I can only feel
disgust and abhorrence. . .Does it make much sense if I write
a thirteenth or fourteenth volume [of the *Church Dogmatics*]
after I was not able to stop the breakthrough of this flood
with the preceeding twelve volumes? Do we not need other
newer voices to bring it to a halt. . .while I sit at a small
table in the corner smiling in a friendly and crafty way,
knowing everything in fact better, even respectfully listened
to, but in the end--not heard?" (p. 82).

His age and health, the ills of friends and relatives,
and sundry disquieting events in theology and politics contributed to his pessimism (p. 476 f). Barth says that such
things taught him patience (p. 258), but most of the forces
behind these moods remain in the background. It is his enjoy-
ment of these years which comes through again and again. Thus,
ever after four months hospital stay in 1965, after which he
had to wear a bothersome catheter, his "G-string" (p. 309),
Barth could still remain "thankful to God and to people that I
am alive, am permitted to read, lead discussions, smoke, sing
psalms and chorales, listen to Mozart, enjoy my 14 grandchil-
dren, and in similar positive ways to exist from day to day"
(p. 309).

Whether it was little things like a new desk or more important things like his weekly visits to Charlotte von Kirschbaum or his ecumenical activity, he was always thankful to God
and to people. Even so, and here the diversity of the volume
is prefigured, his own failure to be thankful enough in the
face of the many gifts given him still bothered him.

Besides the author himself, two other strands of unity in

this volume must be mentioned. First, there are relatively
lengthy exchanges with Hans Küng (12 letters), Ernst Wolf
(10 letters), Carl Zuckmayer (7 letters), Alfred Ernst (6 letters), Helmut Gollwitzer (5 letters), Joseph Hromadka (4 letters), and some others. Particularly striking is the way he
introduces himself to the dramatist Carl Zuckmayer,[4] whom he
comes to see as "a late but all the more thankfully encountered
friend and even younger brother" (p. 416) and whose visits
Barth awaited with an almost childlike excitement (p. 472).

Further, about two thirds of the correspondence is split
between Germany and Switzerland. Because of the excellent an-
notations of the editors, the volume provides a good commentary on the course of events in these two countries during the
1960's. (Obviously, most of the letters are in German, although there are six letters in French and eight in English.)
The importance of Barth's "dual citizenship" (p. 311) is
clearly reflected in his decisions to speak out or to be si-
lent on issues ranging from nuclear armaments and the death
penalty to relations with East Germany. Not surprisingly,
Barth sees "the process of disintegration in Evangelical theology" closely connected to these and other struggles for the
commonweal since World War II (p. 54) and even World War I
(p. 51, p. 298). His view of the theological scene in these
lands can be traced through the letters which constitute nothing short of brief book reviews of the major texts of the
1960's. For example, he writes critical letters to Küng,
Moltmann, and Pannenberg and more positive reactions to books
(on himself!) by Ulrich Hedinger (p. 63 f), B. A. Willems
(p. 131), Martin Storch (p. 246 f), and Friedrich Schmid
(p. 264 f). Thus, the unity of this volume is provided by the
author himself, a few of his addressees, and a geographically
focused political and theological context.

However, these strands of unity must not overshadow the

diversity of the book. Indeed, over and above its unique concentration on Barth's final years, the collection is also unusual because of the multiplicity of people, places, and topics
covered. The previously published epistolary exchanges with
Bultmann and Thurneysen, as well as other correspondence in
preparation for publication, such as letters to Markus and
Christoph Barth, at least have the benefit of singular individuals on the giving and receiving end. This volume provides
little of such unity. In fact, the editors have made the collection "as complete as possible" and have preferred to print
"too much rather than too little"; they also point out, however, that "absolute completeness" in the selection of letters
from these years is impossible for a variety of reasons. As
far as I can see, no final evaluation of their principles of
selection can be ventured until we see what future letters to
be published reveal, including, the editors promise, another
volume like the present one (p. xxiii f).

The diversity is of several sorts. The documents range
in length from letters, which comprise almost three fourths of
the collection and extend from one to over seven pages, to
brief handwritten postcards. Over half of the letters and
cards are isolated responses, including most of the two dozen
anonymously addressed letters. Three fourths of the letters
are signed with a variant on the formal mode of address. Barth
wrote to nieces and old friends, pastors and widows, politi-
cians and a pope, prisoners and theologians from California to
Indonesia and the Netherlands to Sicily; he wrote on topics
ranging from his own state of mind and body to gossip and commentary on local and international politics, culture, and ecclesial events.

There simply is no way to find a common denominator to
this diversity. However, some examples might suggest the variety of people and causes addressed. To young women he offers

advice "as an experienced fighter in this field" on their future relationship with men: act responsibly and make no hasty
decisions (p. 469 f). To a childhood sweetheart and another
friend having financial cares he sends money with a good-
humoured note (pp. 105, 140, 199). He not only chides a
fellow-theologian for an individualism that has forgotten religious socialism, but offers to visit him to help remedy his
painful loneliness (p. 112 f). To Pope Paul, whose attention
to Barth in sickness and health obviously impressed Barth, he
writes about matters ranging from the Second Vatican Council
to *Humanae Vitae* (pp. 432 ff, 462 ff, 499 ff). He can feel a
deep comradeship with those whom the conditions of finitude
permit no sustained interaction (p. 518). He also knows that
he must sometimes be regretfully content with the fact that
some friendships must remain undeveloped for reasons creatures
cannot fathom (pp. 266, 539). Finally, he would like wind-
instruments to substitute for church-organs, but would prefer
first abandoning the baptism of infants, elsewhere called "a
marginal problem" (p. 143) and introducing the Lord's Supper
on a weekly basis (p. 489).

Such diversity is, of course, endemic to the epistolary
genre, especially when the addressees and topics covered are
so broad. Indeed, the diversity is perhaps one reason for
Barth's ambiguous attitude toward letter writing. He regretted
any unanswered letters (e.g. pp. 105, 155, 252 f), but he
could also report in 1967 that "a little [literary] production
is occasionally still possible, especially in the form of abun-
dant correspondence with persons whom I consider especially
suitable or even in need of it; trivial correspondence is, interestingly enough, much more difficult for me. . ." (p. 409;
cf. pp. 196, 228, 293).

However, I also think that the diversity of the material
offered here, both serious and trivial, is its own lesson. In

the first place, such diversity means that these letters will
be of interest to a broad range of people, from historians interested in Barth's ad hoc reading of the recent past to theologians looking for his summary remarks on a Rahner or a Moltmann, the Lord's Supper or eschatology.

In the second place, the diversity reminds a '*Gesamtausgabe*-generation' of the multilayered character of this man and
his cause. This generation does not, to generalize a point
once made by Grover Foley with reference to some Roman Catholic readings of Barth,[5] live in the 'dark ages' in their use
of Barth; that is, it knows that polemical responses to Barth
are insufficient and will ultimately only yield that indifference which is not unheard of nowadays. But neither does
this generation live in a 'golden age' which can easily digest
the whole and enjoy the richness before adding what have become clichéd qualifications. There are some, both friends and
enemies of "Barthology" (p. 374), who lay claim to the key to
the whole of Barth's theology, context, and character, but the
variety of people and topics addressed in this volume seems to
challenge all such attempts. The diversity of interests Barth
had and satisfactions he pursued seem to overwhelm any grid
which would render the matter simple. The web of public and
private affairs in the letters is irreducibly complex, at
least until students have more time to sift patiently the materials in volumes like this one.

It is this unity-in-diversity that makes for the exciting
but complicated spectrum of possibilities presented here and,
indeed, by the whole project of a complete edition. How is
one to do justice to one man who so often seemed to want only
to say one thing, but who did this in interaction with so many
diverse people and circumstances? Such is the question this
volume poses, although the letters do not tell one how to hold
together the unity and the diversity.

Barth himself had begun making remarks on this problem considerably before his retirement, but in this collection it is clear that he, too, saw no easy solution. At times he insists that people turn away from his theology and concentrate on doing the job better than he had (e.g. pp. 2, 76, 139, 320, 531). His generation had its opportunity (p. 47) and must now ask itself why it was not more successful instead of standing in the way of a new generation (p. 294). To those who object that this smacks of an 'actualism' which makes all his writing useless, Barth can only caution that no one stands or falls with praise of him; indeed one must not overlook that, as he says, much of his theology was simply motivated by the fact that *he* needed it (p. 4 f). At other times, however, he proudly turns people towards his own theology. This was a theology which might allow for "reconsideration" of certain themes but which was at least approximately on the right track (pp. 64, 377). This even applies to those who complain with "the same old story" that no room has been left for anything really "new" in his unfinished eschatology; Barth saw "nothing" new in any of the alternatives (p. 376 f). Again, at times he directs people toward the social context of his theology (p. 209); on other occasions, however, he directs them away from his theology and its content and toward the "subject matter" he passionately pursued (p. 368).

Barth's suggestions at this point are by no means inconsistent, but the diversity of this volume is a reminder of how important this complex background is for enjoying the richly simple One whom Barth wanted always to be in the foreground. Indeed, it does not seem out of line with either this volume of letters or Barth's own suggestions to propose that it may only be in the movement between such unity and diversity that Barth's character, content, and theology will present the needed challenge to contemporary church and world.

The editors are to be commended for the patience and diligence with which they selected and annotated a collection that is useful both in its diversity and its unity. Working through the serious and the mundane moments of this diversity-in-unity is instructive and encourages one to keep an eye on the amazing project of which it is a part.

NOTES

1. In 1977 TVZ published another collection of letters, the correspondence between Karl Barth and the dramatist Carl Zuckmayer: *Späte Freundschaft Carl Zuckmayer/Karl Barth in Briefen,* Hinrich Stoevesandt, ed., pp. 96. The volume contains 16 letters by Zuckmayer and 8 by Barth, of the latter of which letters 7 are contained in the volume reviewed here. In addition to a foreword, the editor has included a poem by Zuckmayer about "fathers", as a generational, not biological entity. Barth's delightful set of rules for older people in their relation to younger ones, a letter to Eberhard Busch from Zuckmayer and his account of this "late" friendship, composed *in memoriam* of Karl Barth, and a very useful index.

2. The trip to Rome led to the publication of Barth's instructive little book *Ad Limina Apostolorum,* (Zürich, TVZ, 1967). E.T. under the same title, (Richmond, John Knox Press, 1968).

3. (Philadelphia, Fortress Press, 1976). cf. the comprehensive review of this book by Hans Frei at the end of this volume.

4. See Note 1.

5. "The Catholic Critics of Karl Barth," *Scottish Journal of Theology,* vol. 14, 1961, pp. 136-155.

AN AFTERWORD

EBERHARD BUSCH'S BIOGRAPHY OF KARL BARTH

Hans W. Frei

When Friedrich Schleiermacher, the greatest systematic
theologian of the nineteenth century, died, his reputation
went into decline from which it did not fully recover for
two generations. He was overshadowed by the ghost of Hegel,
his rival and antagonist at the University of Berlin. Those
who followed in his own footsteps at the time were for the
most part colorless epigones who reduced his complex and profound thought to a minor, compromising scholasticism. It
wasn't the first or last time that this happened. The truism
is right: A great man condemns the rest of us to the task of
understanding his thought, a job that usually turns out to be
thoroughly thankless, at least in the first decade or so after
his death. Certainly Karl Barth has so far suffered the fate
of his great predecessor. In this country he was identified
with "neo-orthodoxy", and its demise as a result of the radical 60's meant that his own complex, massive reflections were
submerged and left to an array of residual Barthians. There
are signs that he is being read again, but interest in him

*Eberhard Busch, *Karl Barth. His Life and Letters and
Autobiographical Texts,* John Bowden, translator. (Philadelphia, Fortress Press, 1976), pp. viii, 569. An unrevised form
of this review was first published in *The Virginia Seminary
Journal,* July, 1978, 42-46, and is printed here with the permission of that journal. The editor is deeply grateful for
the permission to include this article in this volume.

among mainline Protestants and Catholics still seems at a
rather low ebb.

The publication of Eberhard Busch's biography of Barth is
therefore most welcome. It is not a critical biography but a
story woven together from a pastiche of Barth's own autobiographical snippets, reports and letters--an autobiography at
a second hand. Busch, who was Barth's last assistant puts all
these beads on two strands designed to show them off to maxi-
mum advantage. One is Barth's own persuasion, old-fashioned
and Calvinist one way, almost aesthetic in another, that
earthly life is a pilgrimage with a cumulative pattern built
into it which is only partially evident at any given time.
Busch does his (very good and tactfully muted) best to make
Barth's own life illustrate the thesis. The other strand consists of brief maps of Barth's theology, each corresponding to
a specific stage of his life, so that his theology too becomes
a "pilgrim's progress". This is very well done but for reasons
to be touched on later may be too concentrated and specialized
for those who do not already have some acquaintance with
Barth's writing.

I

This book is obviously only part of the raw material for
an eventual critical biography of Barth. Though it might make
one wistful, it is probably just as well that the appearance
of such an *oeuvre* should be postponed. A colorful, larger-
than-life personality like Barth might tempt a biographer prematurely into writing either a traditional "life," a kind of
adulatory, Victorian character account, or into something like
Lytton Strachey's elegant and skeptical transformation of the
genre into iconoclastic motivational inquiry. Either perfor-
mance would be a disservice, and certainly Barth's own brief

forays into biographical description, for instance in *Protestant Theology in the Nineteenth Century*, indulge neither in hero worship nor in motivational muckraking. One can only hope that his eventual biographer(s) will combine a healthy sense for the significance and power of Barth's accomplishment with some critical distancing tools which would also serve to provide illuminating context, for example, psychobiography or sociobiography. (But he/she had better also be aware of the limitations of these procedures!) But our day is probably too close for that, and this is indeed sad because Barth was an extraordinarily fascinating and complex person about whom one wants to know more. Had he not been a theologian, he would have been more widely recognized as one of the towering minds of the twentieth century. But it is precisely his overpowering quality that makes it necessary to gain some distance from him before one can have the confidence that one has put him in the right critical context. In the meantime Busch's book is a fascinating account, at once preliminary and yet also of abiding value.

Even the judgment of Barth's complexity has to be qualified. Certainly he was complicated and not always genial in his personal relations, in his curious mixture of candor and reserve, self-confidence and self-ironization, sharp polemical thrust and contrasting breadth of imagination and sympathy. But he was forcefully clear, even simple in other respects. His theological purpose was clearly singleminded, and through all his internal revolutions and revisions he exhibits a striking continuity, even though it would be difficult to state it in a way that is neither misleading nor uninformatively flatfooted. As a theological advocate or opponent, as an actor on the public stage, he never left anybody in doubt where he stood on any specific theological, political or economic issue of the day. He often drove toward a logic of extremes, and often the

98

extremes would be simultaneous and mutually contrary. (For
example, Franz Overbeck's atheism and J. C. Blumhardt's conservative eschatological prophecy appealed to him equally and for
the same eschatological reasons in the 1920's.) But sooner or
later he would discover his own position in the dialectical to-
and-fro and defend it with the same tenacity that had gone into the labor of discovery. He was definitely not one ever to
be pulled here and there "on the boundary," theologically, politically or in personal life. He was decisive, and could be
frustratingly, even infuriatingly contrary and stubborn.
Busch reports that on one occasion the church historian Hans
von Campenhausen "quivered with anger because Karl Barth gave
his political views in such a way that those who differed were
necessarily put in question" (p. 405). This was over Barth's
vehement opposition in 1954 against Adenauer's and the Eisen-
hower Administration's policy of rearming West Germany.

In short, what comes through in this autobiography-at-
second-hand is an astonishingly strong, forceful personality,
at once complex and yet extraordinarily singleminded in the
work he considered important. Again and again, Busch spot-
lights Barth's complete dedication to his vocation, dogmatic
theology, as his particular service within the Christian community, the church. That was obviously his primary community,
even if he was also passionately, if to some extent skeptical-
ly, engaged in political society, and to a lesser extent in
the life of culture. When he wasn't working at his academic
chores he was active in church life and in the world of affairs.
He was constantly, though apparently not frenetically, engaged:
One is not surprised to learn from the *Church Dogmatics* that
Barth, unlike most other modern theologians, put sloth as high
as pride on his list of sins. In this, as in many other ways,
he was very much the Reformed Churchman, a species that has not
often been accused of laziness. Reading Busch's book one gets

a sense of deep-rooted and vigorous but thoroughly worldly and always activist rather than contemplative or spiritualistic piety at work. It seems to have been a piety that knew all about its own skepticism or "bad faith," but had put it in back of itself with complete confidence. This kind of temperament was bound to be utterly dismaying to much of the liberal religious sensibility with its critical tentativeness and its fears of professing more than one believes or practises and landing in hypocrisy as a result.

In a parallel fashion one has the impression that Barth was a man for whom overt force of character and the exercise of vocation, rather than internal self-consciousness, self-probing or the tensions of "self-transcendence" were the hallmarks of being human and of his own humanity. (One suspects that he would not have been a very patient subject in psychoanalysis.) Likewise, his relations with others, including many long and loyal friendships with other theologians and pastors, seem to have been forged through a sense of common vocation and common moral tasks, rather than through the art of mutual personal cultivation or direct in-depth "encounter." His intimate relation with his long-time assistant, Charlotte von Kirschbaum, was in its way perhaps the most striking instance of the first type of relationship in his life; his sad misrelation to his wife was his paradigmatic failure in the other kind. Future biographers will have to undertake some exceedingly painful inquiries about these matters. To what extent did a sense of shared vocation govern even his intimately personal, sexual life?

How much perspective Barth had on himself is a difficult question. He was aware of, and sometimes bothered by, the fact that his relations to people, even long-held friendships, could go sour; there is at least one wistful remark that "my life's work sees to lack a certain attraction; indeed, one

characteristic of it seems to be a certain explosive or at any
rate centrifugal effect" (p. 249; cf. p. 229). He seemed to
sense that people felt threatened and overwhelmed by him, and
at least later in life he tried to guard himself and others
against his own forcefulness with an increasingly fatherly attitude. He also tried to ward off the temptations of fame,
including the sycophancy of "Barthians." How successful these
endeavors were is hard to estimate from Busch's account. Certainly, Barth actually relished opposition even though he
could drive opponents to distraction by his confidence that he
was right. Equally surely he was no fanatic, even if he was
headstrong and willful, especially in his younger years. His
protective device against his own, as well as others', preten-
sions was frequent ironization, self-ironization and self-
needling, sometimes in mock-solemn, mock-elevated language.
It is an interesting but double-edged instrument, and it says
much about Barth. People often try to exorcise their all too
real demons by mocking them either in deliberate exaggeration
or in transparently tongue-in-cheek denial. Barth did both.
To a friend reproaching him for always wanting to be right
"he retorted with a chuckle: 'But I always *am* right'" (p.
395). His notoriously vehement polemical pamphlet of 1934
against Emil Brunner (*No! Reply to Emil Brunner*), written at
a time when he was fiercely and combatively tilting with a
whole host of opponents, he introduced with the words: "I am
by nature a gentle being and completely disinclined toward all
unnecessary quarrels." One is reminded of a painfully jocose
and all too revelatory remark by former Israeli Foreign Minister Moshe Dayan to then Secretary of State Cyrus Vance: "Mr.
Secretary, as soon as you accept our position we shall be in
perfect accord." Vance was not amused. Nor were all of
Barth's contemporaries. Ritual exorcism by humor all too often
reaffirms the tenant rights of the very demons seemingly ex-

pelled, especially in the case of forceful personalities.

II

But when all is said and done, Barth's astonishing confidence and ego strength served him well in many ways. They
were in large part a function of a sense of identity so secure
that he could throughout all his life castigate the narrower,
ungenerous parts of the very heritage that helped supply it in
the first place. He was a loyal, but very critically loyal,
Swiss Reformed Churchman all his life, and as such he became a
dedicated citizen of the universal church of Jesus Christ within a world he saw as one in its suffering and promise. More
than anything else the Busch biography is the personal detailing of that life vocation from Barth's perspective, with all
the power of his vigorous personality manifest.

Most readers will find the sections detailing his passion-
ate break with theological liberalism and his equally passion-
ate fight against the inhumanity of the Nazi regime the most
engrossing. To summarize briefly what was at stake in those
battles is impossible. Especially in regard to his epoch-
making break with theological liberalism, between 1915 and
1922, too many factors enter the picture. For example, there
is the part played by Barth's vigorous (and life-long) socialist and anti-imperialist political convictions, fairly unusual for a Protestant minister in Switzerland and certainly
much more so in Germany at the time. At some stages he did,
at others he did not relate them to his theological revolt.
Both in those and later years Barth revised again and again
the rationale of his drastic theological turn. Furthermore
he was at that time writing very much as a theological pastor
to other pastors, passionately and explosively, so that a

thumbnail sketch of his prose is inappropriate to the point of
being misleading.

But one theme, as important as any Barth pursued throughout that period, was that knowledge of and relationship with
God are not a given, natural state of affairs to be confidently
enjoyed and nourished, but a complete crisis in our being. For
this relation is at once inescapable and deeply problematical
because it is embodied not in our strengths and achievements
but in the ultimate and ineluctable limits of our lives and
capacities. In his own very Christian and very individual way
he was stating the general ideological crisis of many Europeans
in the wake of the First World War, which Expressionists and
radical socialists had already presaged in earlier days. Certainly in the famous second edition of his *The Epistle to the
Romans,* Barth's deliberately abrupt and staccato style, his
distended, exaggerated metaphors and the provocative, allusive
force of his rhetoric are all strikingly reminiscent of Expres-
sionism, although he soon abandoned that mode and (once more
astonishingly similar to an identical turn in contemporary
German letters), moved on to the style of a *neue Sachlichkeit.*
In any event, his statement of the crisis was indeed thoroughly
Christian: The crisis of faith, it was important to him to say
is not the effect of our *not* knowing God but, on the contrary,
of the fact that even in our skepticism we cannot get rid of
him. "Don't things get dangerous only *if* and *because* God is?"
(p. 91). Implied is not only that God is inescapable but that
the condition for knowing God, and even knowing that we do *not*
know him, is God himself. In this view even the radical skepticism of "modernity," much as it is to be preferred to liberal
or conservative religious self-confidence or complacency about
divine-human contact, is child's play compared to the absolute
crisis under God, the discovery at the limit of our lives that
the absolutely transcendent is inescapable, and that it is its

ingression upon us through our questioning, and not our own
questioning itself, that makes our whole being a critical problem.

Barth had a hard time expressing this conviction in a way
that suited him theologically, for it contained a basic ambi-
guity that cried out not only for clarification but, even more,
decision. He could move in one of two and only two directions.
He could quite self-consciously be a Christian theologian within the framework of the ideological and cultural crisis of
"modern Western man." In that case his theology would have
become an ambitious endeavor to interpret cultural and ecclesiastical outlooks and communities to each other, trying to
show that Christianity is the ultimate cutting edge of the
radical, *autonomous* quest for meaning and self-understanding
of modern despisers and, for that matter, non-despisers of religion. Not as Christians but simply as finite, yet autonomous human beings we are finally constituted as an insoluble
question to ourselves; and the question that we ourselves are
is at the same time our question about God which we cannot
answer. Of our own momentum we are driven to the desperate
edge of the absolutely transcendent. The interpretation of
Christianity would in that case be constituted by an anthropo-
theology, in which understanding of God and genuinely authentic
human self-understanding would be mutually indispensable,
each being interpreted through the other. Our autonomous,
self-and God-questioning would at the same time be understood
at its radical edge as our being questioned by God.

On the other hand, he could decide that the relation between the self-description of Christianity and all *autonomously* conceived human, cultural quests for ultimate meaning is
indirect, that they are logically diverse even when they are
existentially connected, that is to say, even when they reside
within the same breast. In that case one could not system-

atically correlate the two. This in turn has two consequences.
First, a Christian theologian opting for this alternative
would presumably give priority to Christian self-description,
so that description of the general human condition, whether in
"crisis" or not, would be dependent on that prior description.
From that vantage point, and given that a Christian outlook is
universal in scope, he would therefore not view the quest for
self-understanding or ultimate meaning as an autonomous enterprise at all. Rather, he would refer it strictly to the distinctive judgment and saving grace of God in Jesus Christ as
the sole and encompassing context within which to reflect on
all such matters. But, secondly, he would then in effect
agree with the increasing number of post-Christian "secular-
ists" that the time was past (if indeed it had ever existed)
when Christianity could supply either the symbolic form or the
substantive answer to an *autonomously* conceived cultural, anthropological quest for ultimate meaning and self-understanding.

The whole conceptual scheme or framework of a self-
involving 'question and answer' pattern or of the 'hermeneutical circle' between an existential preunderstanding and the
understanding of the Christian message would then lose its
supposed status as *the* indispensable conceptual or dialectical
instrument for thinking Christianly. . . In some conditions
such talk might be appropriate, in others not. Rather, Christian theology must in the first place pay heed to the language
of the Christian community from the Bible to modernity, understood as an organic pattern possessing its own integrity, its
own complex logic and highly varying relation to other forms
of language and life.

These were the options that Barth's early, anti-liberal
protest opened up to him. His *Romans* commentary and other contemporary writings left the issue unresolved under the apparent

solution that the gospel constitutes the "absolute crisis" of
autonomous secular as well as religious humanity. This rather
broad notion and others like it merely served to veil, to a
surprising degree, the fact that the choice between the two
positions just outlined really cut to the bone. This intellectual confusion was no doubt in part a function of the existentially tough character of the decision that was involved.
Increasingly, painstakingly, and then more and more decisively
Barth opted for the second alternative. Eventually, in the
early 1930's, as his dogmatic theology developed and under the
impact not only of theological but political controversy
against the intrusion of Nazi ideology into the church, he
came to put it in that extraordinary, one-sided, controversial
dogmatic-theological fashion that was to become his hallmark:
Jesus Christ, he said, as witnessed in all of Scripture, is
the one and only Word of God and the only source for the knowledge of God. Here God is present and known to us, and the
only logical presupposition for this presence and this knowledge is--itself. For this unique thing there can be no set
preconditions; it creates its own. No natural theology, no
anthropology, no characterization of the human condition, no
ideology or world view can set the conditions for theology or
knowledge of God. Autonomous anthropology and Christian theology cannot be understood as mutually implicated, nor is there
any one specific conceptual framework that must be *the* precondition for making theological discourse meaningful.

Not only was this thesis vehemently controverted at the
time; all of its forms: that of totally Christ-focused knowledge of God; the logical (though not existential) discontinuity
between such Christocentric theology and an independent anthropology or cultural world view; the dominance of the constancy
of Christological affirmation over the variableness of its
conceptual expressions and anthropological correlations; and

Barth's earlier, apparent taking-for-granted that God is, despite or even in our not knowing him, are largely responsible
for the wide rejection of Barth's thought since his death.
But at the time he set them forth they were expressions of an
enormous theological vitality which became a powerful force on
behalf of an embattled cause.

Theologically and also politically his thesis served as
a rallying point for those who wished to resist firmly the
attribution of even secondary divine "revelatory" status to
the nationalistic fanaticism that took possession of Germany
in 1933 under Hitler. They were a small group, and they needed all the courage they could muster. The great danger to
the Church's witness, as Barth saw clearly, was not the stupid
and fanatical "German Christian movement" which envisioned
Nazism as the fulfillment of Christianity (yes, there actually
were those!) but the compromisers who saw two sources for discerning the will and action of God--the Bible, but also the
historical events of time, nation and culture. Quite naturally
then he reserved his most vehement polemics for those whom he
thought most consistent in compromising the exclusive sovereignty of the divine Word in their dogmatic as well as their
political theology. In dogmatics they asserted the indispensable methodological coherence of autonomous anthropology,
the fruit of reflexive analysis of subjectivity and of contemporary culture, with a biblical doctrine of God's relation to
man. They then quite logically united this dogmatic compro-
mise to a similar political-theological one for which (again)
God made himself known in Scripture but also in the special
vocation, culture and laws of particular nations at particular
times. Concretely, of course, the latter claim meant in 1933
that the German "national renewal" was being acclaimed as divinely sanctioned. The man who represented this compromising
combination most consistently and disastrously in Barth's

view in the early and mid 1930's was his former ally in the earlier days of the "dialectical theology," Friedrich Gogarten. In the face of this sort of thing Barth passionately asserted and reasserted the exclusive sovereignty of the one Word of God, exclusively testified to in Scripture. He asserted and reasserted the indirect identity of the whole Bible, both Old and New Testaments, with the one and only Word of God incarnate in Jesus of Nazareth.

In those days, a small embattled minority took heart not only from the singleminded tenacity and clarity of Barth's thesis but from his boldness (some called it brashness). In 1932, in the preface to the first volume of his *Church Dogmatics,* he said that anyone waiting for the Protestant church to take itself (i.e., its dogmatic-theological task) seriously would have to wait until doomsday, "unless in all modesty he dares in his own place and as well as he knows how, to *be* that church." For a minority voice to assume that it actually represents--not to say embodies--the group in which a majority diverges from him is a bold claim. Barth extended it quite naturally from the dogmatic-theological to the political-theological arena. For him it was all of one piece, given the force of his governing conviction about the sole sovereignty of the Word of God and its compelling character.

The trouble was that others never quite saw matters in the same almost ruthlessly single-minded way; nor could they use in the same fashion the strange-appearing and consistent dogmatic language which Barth now came to employ. Even people who agreed with him in the German church struggle dissented from his theological rationale for his stand. And as time went on and the echoes of that battle (with its arguments over the mystification and demystification of national culture) faded, more and more people rejected Barth's theological insistence that just as there can be no "natural theology" for

Christians, so there can be no systematic "pre-understanding,"
no single, specific, consistently used conceptual scheme, no
independent or semi-independent anthropology, hermeneutics,
ontology or whatever, in terms of which Christian language
and Christian claims must be cast in order to be meaningful.
Despite his eminence and the sheer weight of his presence on
the theological scene, he always remained a curiously isolated
figure. Even if he set the terms of the argument, and to a
large extent he did, most people took the other side, to
which Rudolf Bultmann eventually gave representative expression with his call for an existential pre-understanding and a
consistent conceptual structure, that of Existentialist philosophy, in terms of which to interpret the New Testament message in modern day.

Busch's detailed account, or rather his shaping of Barth's
own fragmentary accounts of the theoretical and practical
struggles from the break with liberalism to the end of the
Second World War, a period of about thirty years, is admirably
done and conveys the spirit and passion of that epoch in theology, politics and Barth's personal life. It makes compelling
reading in the midst of some things that do not. Busch is an
almost painfully conscientious and fair-minded author. Not a
single individual who crossed Barth's path and no event, no
matter how minute, seems to be left out. The index of persons
alone comes to almost twelve double column, small print pages
in the German original. For the American reader these details
of the Swiss and German landscape, theological, ecclesiastical
and academic, are apt to prove burdensome. But this is a minor problem. Perseverance will not really be difficult and
will pay off.

III

There is however another and very large problem about the
book. It was virtually inescapable, so that Busch cannot be
faulted for it. Readers of Barth's *Church Dogmatics* usually
come up with the same experience: Whether one agrees with
Barth or not, and despite the endless repetition of themes and
the stylistic heaviness, much increased by the translation,
which loses the almost colloquial vigor of the German original,
there is an increasingly compelling, engrossing quality to the
material. And it is much more accessible than much modern
theology: Even the technical terms don't lose sight of ordinary language, and Barth possesses astonishing descriptive
powers. But then, as one tries to restate it afterwards the
material dies on one's hands. It can be done, but there is
nothing as wooden to read as one's own or others' restatements
of Barth's terms, his technical themes and their development.
It is as though he had preempted that particular language and
its deployment. For that reason reading "Barthians," unlike
Barth himself, can often be painfully boring.

On the other hand, brief summary reports of what he
wrote are apt to be uninformative to the point of being virtually hermetic, except for those who are already "in" on it.
Busch renders a real service by reporting the development of
Barth's theology at every stage of his life. He is a real ex-
pert and obviously knows the massive material inside out. But
his summary reports are almost always of the hermetic variety,
and there is nothing he could have done about it. Barth's
theology had some persistent, simple themes. But their development was extremely complex and subtle, and therein lies its
power, richness, originality and imaginativeness. (Even

Barth's own occasional brief summaries of his thought tend to
lack the force and persuasiveness of the *Dogmatics*.)

Why the prolixity of the *Church Dogmatics*? Why its peculiar character of being at once accessible and yet so difficult to do justice to in exposition and commentary? Barth was
naturally talkative, and the *Dogmatics* was developed out of
his class lectures. Moreover, he obviously felt an unusual
fascination, even for a theologian, with the sheer beauty, the
sublime fitness and also the rational availability of the *loci*
of Christian dogma. This almost aesthetic passion extended
most especially to the classical themes of Christian doctrine
that tend to get short shrift in modern theology, e.g., the
Trinity, Predestination. In addition, it has to be remembered
that Barth was not a systematic but a dogmatic theologian, so
that the whole substance of Christian theology could for him
be mirrored in a distinct way in every one of its major, quasi-
independent topics. (And that obviously makes for length!)
This is especially true of the doctrines of predestinating
grace (vol. II, 2) and reconciliation (IV, I-IV, 4), but it
was already true of the prolegomena to the whole work, vols.
I,1 and I,2. Despite their vast difference over the possibility of system-building, there are shades here of Hegel, Barth's
favorite philosopher, who also saw everything that is knowable
implied and potentially contained in any single instance of it,
and who also wrote or spoke at inordinate length, as though in-
toxicated by his vision.

But when all is said and done, there is a more important
consideration. Barth was about the business of conceptual description: He took the classical themes of communal Christian
language molded by the Bible, tradition and constant usage in
worship, practice, instruction and controversy, and he restated
or redescribed them, rather than evolving arguments on their
behalf. It was of the utmost importance to him that this com-

munal language, especially its biblical *fons et origo*, which, as we have noted, he saw as indirectly one with the Word of God, had an integrity of its own: It was irreducible. But in that case its lengthy, even leisurely unfolding was equally indispensable. For he was restating or re-using a language that had once been accustomed talk, both in first-order use in ordinary or real life, and in second-order technical theological reflection, but had now for a long time, perhaps more than 250 years, been receding from natural familiarity, certainly in theological discourse. So Barth had as it were to recreate a universe of discourse, and he had to put the reader in the middle of that world, instructing him in the use of that language by showing him how--extensively, and not only by stating the rules or principles of the discourse. In that respect he was almost totally different from the much less fluid and much more exclusively second-order as well as single-conceptual-system procedure of virtually all of his modern colleagues. This is *not* to say that he was basically less consistent than they. The design that governed Barth's manifold and changing procedures remained very much the same from the first volume of *Church Dogmatics* in 1932 onwards. But unlike others, it was of the essence of his design that it could not be stated apart from its specific unfolding or description without losing its force.

At first Barth had employed a linguistic or cognitive model of a very specific kind in the methodological, introductory part of his dogmatic project, where he raised the question of the internal logic governing the use of dogmatic language. The presence of God's Word to humankind, directly in Jesus Christ and indirectly in Scripture and in the church's contemporary preaching, was, he suggested, to be conceived after the fashion of the free self-presentation or self-reiteration of a subject in performative utterance, so that no ultimate self-differentiation could be made between God's self-expressive language, his activity, and himself. God's Word is God himself in the form of his own spiritual speech-act. Faith in or knowledge of that divine presence was likewise a form of spiritual activity or understanding, one that united intellectual comprehension and existential acknowledgment of that present Word with personal trust and obedience to it.

There was no break, no sharp rupture or later retraction between the methodological introduction and the subsequent content of the *Church Dogmatics*. However, Barth's vision and statement of the world of discourse of which he was rendering an account became increasingly and self-consciously temporal rather than cognitivist. It was a world in which time elapsed, and that was of its very essence, so that he had both to proceed diachronically in describing it and take temporality into account in articulating the most appropriate and least distorting methods. He no longer saw the whole range of divine-human commerce, as it is described in the language of the church, simply under the auspices of an "act" of divine self-projection together with its fit apprehension ("revelation"). Rather, both methodologically and substantively that world of discourse could only be described piecemeal fashion, an important reason for his not developing a system and (again) for his prolixity. Its primary first-order depiction was narrative, the narrative originally told in the Old and New Testaments (though unlike Barthians and neo-orthodox theologians he never systematized the Bible into a single "biblical point of view" or a *"Heilsgeschichte"*). This persuasion of a temporal world became increasingly evident in volumes II, 2; III, 1, and IV. Increasingly he incorporated the retelling of biblical narratives, sometimes in the main text (as in IV), sometimes (as in II, 2 and III, 1) in those enormous small print *excursus* in which he handles his exegesis of the Bible, as well as his discussions with past and present conversation partners.

It was as though even the concepts he employed flowed, and we are watching them move in their own medium, as figurations of motion in time. For this purpose Barth employed a variety of devices, of which I can merely mention two. 'Analogy' is an analytical, technical category which he employed increasingly, beginning with his book on Anselm of Canterbury, *Fides Quaerens Intellectum* and the first volume of the *Church Dogmatics*, to help state the mutual fitness, through God's grace, of God and humanity, in other words, their sharing a common narrative. This contrasted with his earlier (1920's) anti-liberal use of the category and procedure called "dialectic," which served as a name for those thought sequences that indicate at once an absolute distance and a completely static as well as largely negative coinherence of God and humanity. Later in Barth's development, "dialectic" instead became an important subordinate device (and formal category) in the service of "analogy," redescribing conceptually and by means of a series of fluid juxtapositions (of figures, images, events, persons, points of view) the teleological, temporal flow of the divine-human relation, of which the New Testament depiction of Jesus Christ gives at once the foundation and the aim. Analogy and dialectic, like all other technical devices, become expressions of his persuasion that that relation is properly and in the first place narrated, that it can indeed be redescribed, but only secondarily and fragmentarily, even though appropriately, and that it cannot in the first place be argued. Barth's theology proceeds by narrative and conceptually descriptive statement rather than by argument or by way of an explanatory theory undergirding the description's real or logical possibility. (Not even the doctrine of predestinating grace [vol. II, 2] serves an all-embracing explana-

tory function, although Barth sometimes and inconsistently
came close to saying so.)

In the process of this fragmentary, piecemeal description
or rediscription of the temporal world of eternal grace, Barth
employs his battery of auxiliary instruments to indicate two
things simultaneously: (1) that this world is a world with
its own linguistic integrity, much as a literary art work is
a consistent world in its own right, one that we can have only
under a depiction, under its own particular depiction and not
any other, and certainly not in pre-linguistic immediacy or
in experience without depiction; but (2) that unlike any other
depicted world it is the one common world in which we all live
and move and have our being. To indicate all this he will use
scriptural exegesis to illustrate his themes; he will do ethics
to indicate that this narrated, narratable world is at the
same time the ordinary world in which we are responsible for
our actions; and he will do *ad hoc* apologetics, in order to
throw into relief particular features of this world by distancing them from or approximating them to other descriptions
of the same or other linguistic worlds. In such cases, and in
very few others, he engages in argument, usually of a highly
dialectical kind, and usually to indicate distance and proximity at the same time. But none of these other descriptions
or, for that matter, argument with them can serve as a "pre-
description" for the world of Christian discourse which is
also this common world, for to claim that it can would mean
stepping outside that encompassing world; and that by definition is impossible.

All of this of course is done in the conviction that this
world of discourse is indeed descriptively accessible. Ever
since his book on Anselm's *Proslogion's* argument for the existence of God, Barth regarded reason as conceptually descriptive effort, as one, though only one, of the legitimate shapes

of faith, the shape taken by the theological endeavor. But
the appropriate ruled language use of that description is irreducible to any other. Hence he thought that while any and
all technical philosophical concepts and conceptual schemes
could be employed in Christian theology, they could only be
used formally: One must remain agnostic about all their material claims to be describing the "real" world, even or especially when these schemes are anthropological and metaphysical in nature; and Barth did among other ones use anthropological and metaphysical schemes in his theology. In order not to
become trapped by his philosophy, it is best for a theologian
to be philosophically eclectic, in any given case employing
the particular "conceptuality" or conceptualities (to put it
in the German mode) that serve best to cast into relief the
particular theological subject matter under consideration.
The subject matter governs concepts as well as method, not
vice versa.

Professor Maurice Wiles once suggested (*The Remaking of
Christian Doctrine*, 1974, pp. 24f) that Barth is best read as
a poet among theologians, much as Arnold Toynbee should be
read as a poet among historians rather than as a historian.
Barth himself spoke relatively infrequently, though most ap-
preciatively, of the use of imagination in theology. But he
knew how to use it, which is more to the point. One is tempted
to speak of his work as the product of "dogmatic imagination,"
if possible pejorative overtones of that awkward construction
may be disallowed in advance. In much the same way as the now
old-fashioned "newer" literary critics he set forth a textual
world which he refused to understand by paraphrase, or by
transposition or "translation" into some other context but interpreted in second-order reflection with the aid of an array
of formal, technical tools. Sometimes the second-order talk
merged with imaginative restatements, in various modes, of

parts of the original narrative to which it is fitly related.
In a sense, then, he was indeed a poet, setting forth mimetic-
ally a world of discourse, but with a clear and strong sense
of the appropriate coinherence of technical theological analysis with its more imaginative counterpart. The two are carefully crafted together, and together they are governed by the
controlling subject matter.

There are many different ways of doing theology, many
controlling concerns and outlooks, and one may not want to
agree with Barth's governing vision, or with his particular
exercise of imagination or of rationality or both together.
But can really strong theology be any less? Can it be less
than *some* form of this combination?

* * * * * * * * * * *

The prolixity and accessibility of Barth's theology, as
well as the difficulty of second-hand restatement, are all
then in the nature of the case. They are functions of the
distinctive, even classic character of Barth's work. But they
forced an impossible task on Eberhard Busch when he tried to
summarize the stages of Barth's theologizing. The enduring
excellence of this book is therefore neither that it gives us
a critical perspective on Barth the man, nor that it succeeds
at a less than highly technical level of joining the theology
to the man. But in between there can be a statement of Barth's
life as his own Christian vocational task, as his pilgrimage.
At that significant level Busch could not have done better.
His care and craftsmanship and the breadth of his work in the
sources are such that his work is not likely to be superseded
in this respect, even by a critical biography.

NOTES ON THE CONTRIBUTORS

JAMES J. BUCKLEY holds a Ph.D. from Yale University. For
several years he taught at the University of Detroit and
is now in the Theology Department of Loyola University in
Baltimore.

EBERHARD BUSCH was assistant to Karl Barth until Barth's death.
He has the Dr. theol. from the University of Basel and is
now serving the congregation at Uerkheim of the Swiss Re-
formed Church. His latest book, published by Chr. Kaiser
Verlag in Munich in 1978 is entitled *Karl Barth und die
Pietisten*.

ARTHUR C. COCHRANE, author of several books, including *The
Church's Confession Under Hitler*, taught for years at
Dubuque and Pittsburgh and is now pursuing his retirement
by teaching at Wartburg Theological Seminary at Dubuque,
Iowa.

MICHEL DESPLAND, a native Swiss and author of *Kant on History
and Religion* and, recently, *La religion en Occident:
Evolution des idées et du vécu*, is professor in the Department of Religion, Concordia University, Montréal.

CHARLES C. DICKINSON, who holds a Ph.D. from the University of
Pittsburgh, has taught in Zaire, and Union Theological
Seminary in Virginia. He is now Director of the Honors
Program and professor of Religion and Philosophy at the
University of Charleston, Charleston, West Virginia.

HANS W. FREI, former Master of Ezra Stiles College at Yale
University, is professor of Religious Studies at Yale
University. His most recent publications are *The Eclipse
of Biblical Narrative* and *The Identity of Jesus Christ*.

PAUL L. LEHMANN, Emeritus Charles A. Briggs Professor of Systematic Theology at Union Theological Seminary, New York,
and author of *The Transfiguration of Politics, Ethics in
a Christian Context*, inter alia, now lives in New York
City in an active retirement: studying and writing.

JAMES P. MARTIN is professor of New Testament Studies and
Principal of Vancouver School of Theology. He holds a
Th.D. from Princeton and is the author of *The Last Judg-
ment in Protestant Theology*.

H.-MARTIN RUMSCHEIDT is professor of Historical Theology at
Atlantic School of Theology in Halifax, Nova Scotia and
author of *Revelation and Theology: An Analysis of the
Barth-Harnack Correspondence of 1923*.

JAMES D. SMART has taught many years at Union Theological
Seminary in New York. The author of *The Divided Mind of
Modern Theology* and translator-editor of *Revolutionary
Theology in the Making* now resides in Toronto.